# The Info-line
# Performance Improvement

MW01245616

An Info-line Collection

*Info-line* is a series of "how-to" reference tools; each issue is a concisely written, practical guidebook that provides in-depth coverage of a single topic vital to training and HRD job performance. *Info-line* is available by subscription and single copy purchase.

ISBN 1-56286-096-8

Library of Congress Catalog Card No. 98-73551

Printed in the United States of America.

**ASTD**

1640 King Street
Box 1443
Alexandria, VA 22313-2043
PH 703.683.8100, FX 703.683.8103
www.astd.org

# The Info-line Guide to Performance Improvement

## An Info-line Collection

**Editor**
Cat Sharpe

**Graphic Production**
Anne Morgan

# Fundamentals of HPI

Issue 9811

# Fundamentals of HPI

## AUTHORS:

**Janice Dent**
827 W. 38th Street
Baltimore, MD 21211
Tel: 410.467.6586
E-mail: janicedent@erols.com

**Phil Anderson**
Strategist
ASTD Market Development
1640 King Street
Box 1443
Alexandria, VA 22313-2043
Tel: 703.683.8114
Fax: 703.683.7259
E-mail: panderson@astd.org

**Editor**
Cat Sharpe

**Associate Editor**
Sabrina E. Hicks

**Production Design**
Anne Morgan

**ASTD Internal Consultant**
Pam Schmidt

# Fundamentals of HPI

Without a doubt, many of the organizations we work for are in need of some improvement. Do any of these examples sound familiar?

*A customer service representative (CSR) at a financial services company does not know what mailings went to the customer, so the customer (who is a little irate at this point) has to inform the CSR of new offerings.*

*The volume of claims at a large insurance company is so astronomical that there is a huge backlog of claims that need to be paid. Customers have to wait months before the company can process their claim.*

*Your non-profit organization has to struggle to get anything done, and it seems as if one person is doing all of the work.*

*The programmers at a software company continually produce programs that do not meet the customers' needs.*

Examine what is wrong with your organization:

- Are you losing market share?
- Are you losing customers?
- Are you losing money?

Which of the following do you think will solve your organization's problems:

- more or better information
- the right people in the right jobs
- additional resources
- more motivated employees
- better incentives
- more highly skilled employees

Most organizations seem to take the "one size fits all" approach to addressing their organization's performance problems: **TRAINING.** The problem with haphazardly applying this approach is that training is the right answer only when the problem is caused by a lack of knowledge or skills. A clear understanding must exist that training does not solve problems associated with any of the following:

- inadequate information
- hiring the wrong person for the job
- old, out-dated tools and resources
- poorly designed incentive programs
- poor processes

But what if you had an objective, systematic way to fix what is wrong with your organization? There is a way: human performance improvement (HPI).

This issue of *Info-line* provides you with a detailed explanation of the HPI process and model. What follows is an overview of the roles associated with HPI and a description of the core competencies required of practitioners who want to join this very exciting and rewarding movement. Finally, this issue offers an overview for making the transition from trainer to HPI consultant.

## Defining Performance

Imagine that you have just returned from attending a concert or play. When asked if you enjoyed the event, you reply, "It was good." What do you really mean by this statement? Do you want it understood that the musicians, actors, and support staff were talented or that the basic sheet music or script was entertaining? Or is it that the musicians or actors worked together with the proper leadership from the conductor or the director to produce something that you thought was valuable (and that is why you were willing to spend your hard-earned money on expensive tickets)?

Performance is about factors such as culture, mission, workflow, goals, environment, knowledge, and skills all working together to produce something that is valuable to the consumer. So performance, regardless of the organization that produces the performance (be it a baseball team, software company, girl scout troop, or law firm), is about *outputs* or *results*.

## Three Levels of Performance

Optimal
Performance

Organization

Process

Individual

*Adapted from* Improving Performance:
How to Manage the White Space on the Organizational Chart
*by Geary Rummler and Alan Brache, 1995.*

When the sheet music or the script has potential, but the musicians or actors just are not talented, the performance fails. Perhaps the musicians or actors are talented individuals, but they just are not working well together. The performance just was not "good." Performance, therefore, needs to occur on many levels. Geary Rummler, author and well-known performance specialist, suggests that performance needs to occur on three levels:

1. The performer.

2. The process.

3. The organization.

Optimal performance is obtained when all three levels work in harmony. The *Three Levels of Performance* figure shown at left presents a visual rendition of this process. A breakdown at any one of the levels will prevent optimal performance, thereby requiring some type of planned action to improve performance.

According to Rummler, the organizational level establishes the necessary circumstances for the other levels of performance. When performance is not optimal, examine first the organization's culture, policies, mission, goals, and operating strategies. These factors delineate the boundaries by which we define processes and jobs.

The process level is where the actual work gets accomplished. When performance is not optimal, examine factors such as workflow, job design, required inputs and outputs, and the performance management procedures to see if these processes actually work and support the organizational goals.

The individual performers within the organization affect the processes. When performance is not optimal, determine if the individual performance goals, knowledge and skill, work environment, availability of support tools, coaching, and feedback support the processes.

Seldom is it true that only one set of factors (organization, process, or performer) are adversely affecting performance. When trying to identify why the performance problem exists, it is critical, therefore, to examine factors at all three levels of performance.

The reason for having a performance improvement need within an organization can usually be linked to one of the following three "trigger events":

1. Inadequate performance.

2. Introduction of something new (for example, a new process, system, technology, employee, or law).

3. Increased expectations.

# What is Human Performance Improvement?

The concept of human performance improvement (HPI) or human performance technology is not new. In fact, much of the work that is the basis for the current focus on HPI was conducted in the late 1960s and early 1970s by individuals such as Thomas Gilbert, Joe Harless, Robert Mager, and Geary Rummler.

Much like instructional systems development (ISD) is a systematic process used to design and develop training programs, HPI is a systematic process used to address poor performance. In ASTD's publication *Models for Human Performance Improvement,* author William Rothwell states:

> HPI is the systematic process of discovering and analyzing important human performance gaps, planning for future improvements in human performance, designing and developing cost-effective and ethically justifiable interventions to close performance gaps, implementing the interventions, and evaluating the financial and non-financial results.

**Systematic** means that HPI is approached in an organized, rather than incidental way. It is based on open systems theory, or the view that any organization is a system that absorbs such environmental *inputs* as people factors, raw materials, capital, and information; uses them in such transformational *processes* as service delivery or manufacturing methods; and expels them as *outputs* such as finished goods or customer services. *Process* is a continuous activity carried out for a purpose.

**Discovering and analyzing** means identifying and examining present and possible future barriers that prevent an organization, process, or individual from achieving desired results. *Important* implies that priorities are established in the search for improvement opportunities. Importance is influenced by quantity, quality, cost, time, moral or ethical values, or some combination of these elements.

**Human performance** "denotes a quantified result or a set of obtained results, just as it also refers to the accomplishment, execution, or carrying out of anything ordered or undertaken, to something performed or done, to a deed, achievement, or exploit, and to the execution or accomplishment of the work" according to Harold Stolovitch and Erica Keeps in their book, *Handbook of Human Performance Technology.* Note that the quantifier *human* should be placed in front of *performance* to distinguish it from machine, capital, stock, or other forms of performance. *Gaps* are the differences between actual and desired results in the past, present, or future.

**Planning for future improvements** in HPI is meant to emphasize that HPI work is not focused solely on solving past or present problems; rather, it also can be focused on averting future problems or realizing improvement opportunities.

**Designing and developing cost-effective** and ethically justifiable interventions means finding and formulating optimal or desirable ways of solving past or present human performance problems or planning for future HPI opportunities. The word intervention implies a long-term, evolutionary, and progressive change effort. *Cost-effective* implies sensitivity to bottom-line improvements by those who perform HPI work. *Ethically justifiable* implies sensitivity to ethical and moral viewpoints.

**Implementing the interventions** means finding the optimal—most cost efficient and cost effective—way to plan for HPI. Sometimes called *deployment*, it refers to the installation process for an HPI intervention.

**Evaluating the results** focuses on accountability. Those who do HPI work must always remain keenly aware of the need to gather persuasive evidence of the economic and non-economic value of their efforts.

*Adapted from* ASTD Models for Human Performance Improvement *by William Rothwell, 1996.*

Inadequate performance results when part of the system breaks down. The organizational level is not producing the structure by which processes can be established. Or, the performers are not able to perform the processes.

Examples can include the following:

- Claims are processed incorrectly.
- The product breaks after the third use.
- The answers provided to customers are wrong.
- Deadlines are missed.

When something new is added or will be added to the organization, a performance opportunity exists. The new factor may affect the organizational, process, or performer level of performance.

Examples include the following:

- A new software package is installed.
- A new employee is hired.
- A new law is passed.

In our competitive work environments, today's acceptable performance is tomorrow's unacceptable performance. The organization that proactively identifies the need for an increase in performance will be the organization that beats out its competition.

Examples of proactive behavior include the following:

- Raising quality standards to out perform the competition.

- Increasing sale levels in anticipation of a new rival entering the market.

- Increasing production levels in preparation for launching a new product.

In each circumstance, whether inadequate performance, the introduction of something new, or increased expectations, the HPI process is the same.

# The HPI Process Model

If you think of the performance improvement process in the context of your own health, it is easy to understand. When you are not feeling well and you go to the doctor, the physician asks you a number of questions and runs some tests to determine the cause of the problem. Once the cause is established, the physician selects the right treatment and prescribes it. Sometimes the treatment is simple ("take this pill"), but often the treatment involves many steps ("take this pill, drink plenty of fluids, and get plenty of rest").

Once you begin the treatment, you start to feel better. The doctor may even ask you to look for signs of improved health: "If you don't see a noticeable improvement in two to three days, call me—we could be on the wrong track." As a final step, the doctor sets up a follow-up appointment to ensure that your condition no longer exists. The physician may even order additional tests to compare against the original test.

HPI involves the same steps employed by the doctor. The HPI Process Model (refer to the diagram at right) illustrates the six-step process:

1. Performance Analysis.

2. Cause Analysis.

3. Intervention Selection.

4. Intervention Implementation.

5. Change Management.

6. Evaluation of Results.

## Step 1: Performance Analysis

The performance improvement process starts with a two-step analysis phase. Imagine that when you walk into the examining room the doctor takes one look at you and says, "You have an ulcer." Sounds ludicrous. Why then, in the business environment, do we tend to make quick judgements in our organizations? Look at a simple example:

*Sales manager to training manager: "Four of my sales people didn't meet their sales goals last quarter and I would like to send them to sales training."*

## HPI Process Model

The arrows between the steps in the model represent the system-aspects (inputs and outputs) of the process. For example, the output of the Performance Analysis phase is the input for the Cause Analysis phase.

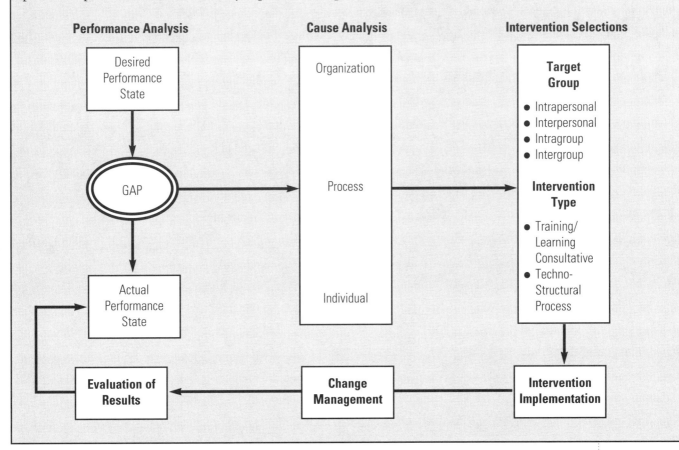

Training manager: *"Didn't we just send all of your people to sales training six months ago?"*

Sales manager: *"Yes, and these four attended that training, but ever since we introduced that new product, they haven't been doing real well."*

Training manager: *"Well how about we just send them to a refresher course. It shouldn't take as long, and it will be a lot cheaper."*

Sales manager: *"Sounds good. I can't afford to have them out of the office for an entire week anyway. Let me know when it is scheduled."*

As an HPI specialist you should ask yourself, "How do we know that training is the right answer to the performance problem unless we ask some questions? Listed below are some sample questions to help you get started:

- Do the sales people have the information they need to sell the new product?

- Have the sales people been given new performance goals that emphasize selling the new product?

- What is the sale person's level of knowledge about the new product?

- What incentives or disincentives are there for selling the new product?

# Cause Analysis: Using a Fishbone Diagram

Follow these instructions to use a fishbone diagram for cause analysis.

**1.** Assemble stakeholders (individual workers, managers, division heads, executives, and so forth).

**2.** Draw this fishbone diagram on a flipchart or whiteboard.

**3.** Have stakeholders describe the performance gap in the box shown on the far right. Have stakeholders clarify what is actually happening (what can be seen and measured) and what results are desired.

**4.** Brainstorm causes of the gap by considering each performance category described in the boxes to the left of the performance gap box. (You will notice that the "bones" on the top of the diagram focus on the individual. The bottom-left "bones" focus on the process and the bottom-right "bones" focus on the organization.)

**5.** Ensure the group that there are no right or wrong answers. Challenge stakeholders to consider all the "bones."

**6.** Record their responses to uncover causes of the performance gap.

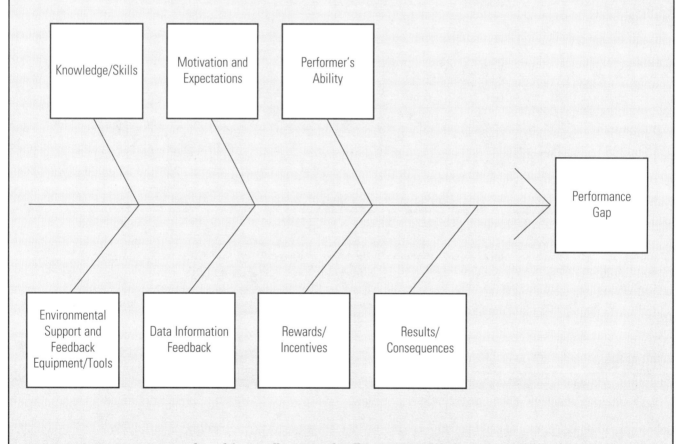

*Adapted from William J. Rothwell's* ASTD Models for Human Performance Improvement *and Tom Gilbert's* Behavioral Engineering Model.

Think of all the money that organizations waste on training, reorganization, or any other intervention because management thought it could not afford to spend the time and money to properly analyze the situation in the first place.

When conducting a performance analysis, you identify and describe past, present, and future human performance gaps. You collect information from key stakeholders (for example, executives, department heads, and line managers) as well as individual performers by asking questions that examine how existing performance compares to the desired performance. Then, you examine documents (such as annual reports or customer surveys) to find the consequences of the performance gap.

Other names for this phase—"performance gap analysis" or "up-front analysis"—refer to the same activity. As with any analysis, you can select a variety of methods to collect the information (such as surveys, interviews, or focus groups). Refer to *Info-lines* No. 9408, "Strategic Needs Analysis" and No. 8502, "Be a Better Needs Analyst" to acquire more information on how to conduct a needs analysis.

You will need to answer the following questions as a result of the performance analysis:

- What is the desired performance situation versus the actual situation?

- What is the gap or difference between the actual and desired performance?

- Who is affected by the performance gap? Is it one person, a group, an organization, or a work process?

- When and where did the performance gap first occur, or when is it expected to begin?

- When and where were the symptoms and the consequences of the performance gap first noticed?

- What has the performance gap cost the organization? Can the impact of the performance gap be measured?

The output of the performance analysis phase is a clearly defined problem or opportunity—complete with the existing and desired conditions that sur-

round performance. You may have also noticed that some of the questions presented to ask during the performance analysis are key to evaluating the success of the HPI process. You need to collect concrete examples of the consequences of the performance gap to measure the effects of the HPI process.

## Step 2: Cause Analysis

Once you have adequately defined the performance gap, you can determine the cause of the gap through a cause analysis. Your goal is to answer one question: Why does the performance gap exist?

You are not simply addressing symptoms; you are getting to the root cause of the gap. First, you need to ask important questions that examine issues related to the organization, the process, and the performer. These questions should include the following issues:

- incentives
- flow of information
- equipment
- employee abilities
- motivation
- work environment
- knowledge and skills

Similarly, you will need to gather your information through a variety of methods. One cause analysis technique uses a *fishbone diagram*. Refer to the diagram at left for instructions on how to use this analysis technique.

Following are the types of questions you will need to answer as a result of a cause analysis:

- How well do performers see the results of what they do?

- How well are performers rewarded or provided with incentives for performing as desired?

- Are performers penalized for achieving desired work results?

# Types of Interventions

| Intervention Types | Possible Causes |
| --- | --- |
| **Training Interventions**<br>Activities that focus on the acquisition of new knowledge and skills. | • lack of knowledge and skills |
| **Consultative Interventions**<br>Activities that focus on helping clients to help themselves. | • lack of support and feedback<br>• lack of results and consequences<br>• performance ability |
| **Techno-Structural Interventions**<br>Activities that focus on the performer's physical setting, available tools, or organizational structure. | • lack of rewards and incentives<br>• lack of equipment and tools<br>• environment support through organization structure<br>• performer's ability |
| **Process Interventions**<br>Activities that focus on how the performers complete their work. | • environmental support<br>• ineffective job/process<br>• design<br>• lack of data information |

## Examples

- classroom training
- on-the-job training
- computer-based training
- web-based training
- job aids
- paper-based self-study
- video-based training

## Partners

- subject matter experts
- line supervisors, managers, executives
- technical writers
- programmers
- workers
- communication specialists
- instructional designers

---

- formal and informal coaching programs
- feedback systems
- mentoring programs
- recognition programs
- reward systems
- incentive plans
- career counseling centers
- career ladders
- tuition reimbursement
- job rotation
- promotion systems

- line supervisors, managers, executives
- HR specialists, generalists, and managers
- survey design experts
- communication specialists
- compensation specialists
- organization development experts
- employee development staff
- career development specialist

---

- ergonomic improvements
- work space redesign
- equipment upgrade
- electronic performance support systems
- re-organization
- employee selection
- information systems
- policies and procedures

- line supervisors, managers, executives
- HR specialists, generalists, managers
- technology specialist
- information systems staff
- ergonomists
- communication specialists
- recruiters and staff specialists
- workflow specialists
- organization development experts
- employee development staff
- career development specialist

---

- job redesign
- competency modeling
- quality systems
- documentation systems
- communication systems
- management systems
- team interventions

- line supervisors, mangers, executives
- workers
- HR specialists, generalists, managers
- team building experts
- information systems staff
- procedures writers
- communication specialists
- strategists
- workflow specialists
- quality control experts
- organization development experts
- employee development staff

- Do the performers have the ability to do the job?

- Are performers given the data, information, or feedback they need to perform at the time they need it?

- Do performers have the support tools and resources they need?

The output of the cause analysis phase is a clearly defined cause or list of causes that you can address by selecting and implementing the appropriate performance intervention. Also, you need to make sure that you have a clear sense of the target group that is involved in the cause.

## Step 3: Intervention Selection

After determining root causes of the performance problem or performance opportunity, you must select the interventions that will address the situation. According to Wendell French and Cecil Bell in *Organizational Development: Behavioral Science Interventions for Organization Improvement*, an intervention is "a set of structured activities in which selected organizational units (target groups or individuals) engage in a task or a sequence of tasks where the task goals are related directly or indirectly to organizational improvement."

Before starting, determine the depth to which you will attack the problem or opportunity. Most performance problems or opportunities exist on several levels (organization, process, or performer). As you delve deeper, the potential benefits increase but so do the risks. Do not tackle more than you can deliver. In addition, you need to keep in mind that most performance improvement requires a combination of interventions.

To address the performance situation, you may need to implement a series of interventions. Perhaps you need an intervention for each of the following situations:

- to establish performance
- to maintain the established performance
- to extinguish incorrect performance

Begin the intervention selection process through divergent thinking. First, list all of the interventions that you can think of that might solve the root cause of the performance gap. Refer to the

*Types of Interventions* chart on the previous pages for a categorized list of possible interventions. At this point in the process, do not worry about how plausible these interventions are—just make sure the intervention addresses the cause. Be sure to relate possible interventions to the target group. For example, if the target group is an individual, do not list interventions that only work with groups. (See the chart *Target Groups* sidebar at right.)

Next to the possible interventions, note the following elements associated with each:

- costs
- benefits
- potential obstacles

Also try to find opportunities where one intervention might solve two or more root causes of the problem. Always consider the organization's culture: which interventions could be effective without disrupting too many of the organization's norms and values? Pare down the list by eliminating ideas that have very little chance of success or are prohibitively expensive. Do not be too hasty—sometimes the craziest ideas start to have merit when considered carefully. At the end of the selection process, be sure that you have selected at least one intervention for each of the root causes.

Answer the following questions that result from the intervention selection process:

- What will a successful intervention be able to do?

- What are the costs and benefits associated with each intervention?

- Will one intervention address more than one cause?

- What are the concerns of stakeholders towards these interventions?

- What will be required to gain buy-in?

- How well do these interventions match what you know about the organization's culture?

The output of the intervention selection phase is a design document that includes intervention requirements, intervention components, and intervention specifications. You will need an action plan that lists the major tasks included for each intervention, the resources required to implement each intervention, and a plan for incorporating stakeholder support.

## Step 4: Intervention Implementation

At this point, you are ready to help the organization implement the selected intervention. Implementation involves four parts: intervention, organization, leadership, and individuals affected.

### ■ *Intervention*

During the implementation phase, watch how people within the organization respond to the intervention. Observe for the following:

- Is it easy to implement? If not, you may need to find a way to implement it in stages.

- Is the intervention similar to past practices? You need to find a way to communicate the similarities to past success stories.

- Can the intervention be modified? Users like to make something their own. A successful implementer does not care if the user makes slight changes to the intervention, as long as it is still effective.

- Does the intervention have any social impact? Users do not want their relationships with other people to change. If it requires change, you will want to communicate these changes early.

### ■ *Organization*

An intervention will be successful only if the organization is ready for it. Prior to full blown implementation, look for the following:

- Are the interventions and the organization's culture in synch? If not, be prepared to fail.

- Does the strategic plan support the intervention? If so, communicate the similarities. If not, stop implementation until you find a way that it can.

- Are there external conditions that will influence the organization negatively? If so, consider postponing the implementation until you are prepared to deal with the external conditions.

## Target Groups

| Target Group | Intervention Examples |
|---|---|
| **Intrapersonal** <br> The performance is the function of an individual. | • career counseling <br> • training <br> • work space redesign |
| **Interpersonal** <br> The performance is a function of the interaction of two or more individuals. | • job rotation <br> • conflict resolution <br> • role clarification |
| **Intragroup** <br> The performance is a function of the interaction amount of team and group members. | • team building <br> • process re-design <br> • rewards systems |
| **Intergroup** <br> The performance is a function of the interaction of two or more groups. | • process clarification <br> • re-organization <br> • strategic planning |

### ■ *Leadership*

Organizational leadership can make or break an intervention. Perhaps the most important aspect of the implementation effort is the sponsor. When identifying and selecting a sponsor, look for someone who fits the following description:

- has the power to validate change within an organization

- is well-respected in the organization and believes in the suggested changes

- has the time to support the effort by writing letters, kicking-off training sessions, providing rewards for good performance, and so forth

- is someone you are comfortable working with— if he or she is not appropriate, you should be prepared to find another sponsor

## What's Your Perspective?

| Training Perspective | Performance Perspective |
| --- | --- |
| **Assumptions** | **Assumptions** |
| Training (giving employees more skills, knowledge, and abilities) is the solution to performance problems. | Training is one possible intervention when there are performance problems or opportunities. |
| The goal of training is to give employees more skills, knowledge, or ability. | The goal of performance improvement is to meet organizational performance goals. |
| A training department should deliver the training that customers ask for. | A performance improvement department should question whether training is needed. |
| A trainer's most important skill is to deliver training and facilitate learning. | A performance consultant's most important skill is to diagnose performance problems. |
| **Roles** | **Roles** |
| Training needs analysis | Performance analysis |
| Training design | Cause analysis |
| Training delivery | Intervention selection and implementation |
| Evaluation | Change management |
| Training management and coordination | Evaluation of results and feedback |
| | Project management |
| **Tools** | **Tools** |
| Assessment instruments | Organization's operating plan |
| Instructional design models | Strategy statement |
| Group process | Annual report |
| Classroom | Survey instruments |
| Learning technology | Process maps |
| Textbooks, workbooks, tests | Templates, models, matrices |
| **Customers** | **Customers** |
| Learner | Process owner |
| Learner's manager | Performer |
| Training purchaser | Performer's manager |
| | Organization's customers |

*Adapted from ASTD's Web site*: www.astd.org.

■ *Individuals Affected*

Finally, you need to consider the individuals affected by the intervention. Below are some items for consideration:

- Some people adapt to change more quickly than others.

- You need to understand the characteristics of your audience to implement an intervention successfully.

- Are other changes occurring at the same time? If too many things are happening at once, you may need to change your time frames.

Note, however, that you are not necessarily responsible for implementing the selected intervention. Your responsibility is to identify the talent and resources needed to implement the interventions. The individuals who actually implement the intervention may be people within your organization (such as members of the human resources department, subject matter experts [SMEs], managers, or trainers). Or, you may get the help of outside consultants who specialize in compensation, ergonomics, management development, or computer programming.

The output of the intervention implementation phase is the occurrence of the actual intervention, such as the following examples:

- a new organizational structure
- an updated software program
- an incentive system
- a training program

A well-planned implementation is necessary for you to track the changes taking place as a result of your efforts.

## Step 5: Change Management

During the change management phase, identify how people are reacting to the intervention, and address these reactions. Some things to consider are as follows:

- Although change management is positioned late in the HPI model, it is critical to begin thinking about change issues very early in the process.

● It is not necessary to have 100 percent of the population in favor of the change. It is actually beneficial to have some doubters.

● All of the planning in the world will not eliminate the discomfort associated with change that results from implementing interventions. As change agent, you need to anticipate the discomfort and make plans on how to address the discomfort.

Diane Dormant, in *Introduction to Performance Technology,* suggests incorporating the following change management strategies:

● Be a spokesperson for the change. Write newsletter articles or create other media events that introduce the change.

● Be credible and positive about the change. Enlist the help of the sponsor or key stakeholders.

● Empathize with the change concerns of the target group. Answer their questions and provide clear, reliable information.

● Emphasize the strengths of the intervention and its changes, and acknowledge the weaknesses too. Again, enlist the help of the sponsor or key stakeholders.

● Provide success images through relevant examples or successful demonstration of the change. If possible, promote discussion with others who have successfully changed.

● Provide incentives or rewards for changed behavior.

● Provide feedback and status reports as reinforcement and support for the change.

Many models represent the stages people go through as they experience change. Several *Info-line* issues address the change management process. Refer to *Info-line*s No. 9715, "The Role of the Change Manager," and No. 8910, "Managing Change," if you need additional help in managing your change effort.

The output of the change management phase is an on-going status report that tracks the following items:

● how well the intervention is working

● effect of the intervention on the target group

● modifications made to the original plan to address new concerns

## Step 6: Evaluation of Results

During the final phase of the HPI process, determine how well the intervention met its desired outcome. To do this, you need to evaluate the intervention itself and the overall performance problem or opportunity. As with the change management phase, it is critical that you begin thinking about evaluation issues very early on in the process. Below are some issues to think about when focussing on evaluation:

● Be sure you are measuring against valid business results. An "increase in employee moral" is not a business result. A 10 percent decrease in production errors is a business result.

● Be sure you identify the desired business results prior to intervention selection.

● Be sure that the date you need to conduct your evaluation is available to you before you agree on how the intervention will be evaluated.

● An obvious link should exist between the selected intervention, the optimal performance, and the desired business result.

● Focus your HPI evaluation on the higher levels of Donald Kirkpatrick's four levels of evaluation (namely, reaction, learning, behavior, and results).

As with analysis, much has been written about training evaluation. If you need additional help with your evaluation efforts, you may want to refer to other *Info-line* issues (such as No. 9801, "Benchmarking"; No. 9705, "Essentials for Evaluation"; No. 9813, "Level 1 Evaluation"; No. 9814,

# HPI Process, Roles, and Skills

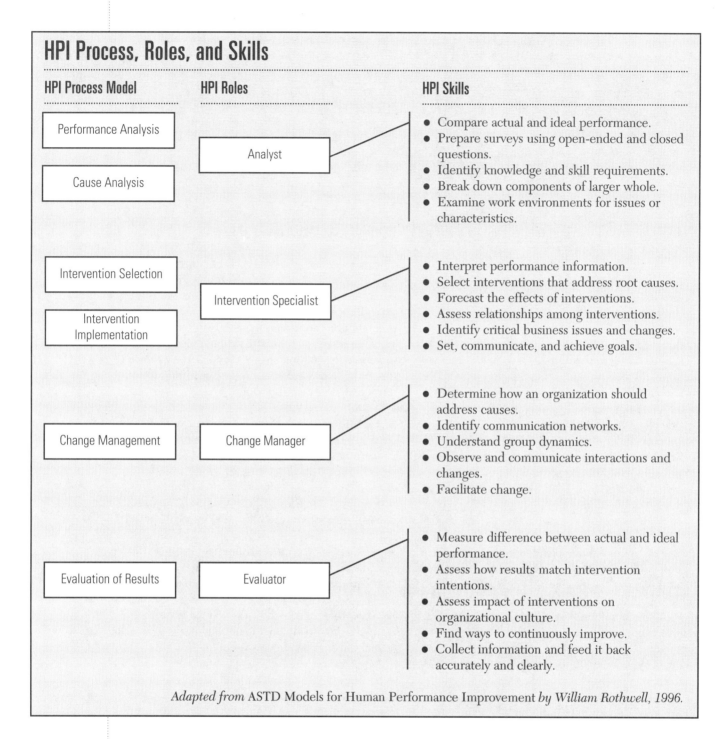

| HPI Process Model | HPI Roles | HPI Skills |
|---|---|---|
| Performance Analysis<br><br>Cause Analysis | Analyst | • Compare actual and ideal performance.<br>• Prepare surveys using open-ended and closed questions.<br>• Identify knowledge and skill requirements.<br>• Break down components of larger whole.<br>• Examine work environments for issues or characteristics. |
| Intervention Selection<br><br>Intervention Implementation | Intervention Specialist | • Interpret performance information.<br>• Select interventions that address root causes.<br>• Forecast the effects of interventions.<br>• Assess relationships among interventions.<br>• Identify critical business issues and changes.<br>• Set, communicate, and achieve goals. |
| Change Management | Change Manager | • Determine how an organization should address causes.<br>• Identify communication networks.<br>• Understand group dynamics.<br>• Observe and communicate interactions and changes.<br>• Facilitate change. |
| Evaluation of Results | Evaluator | • Measure difference between actual and ideal performance.<br>• Assess how results match intervention intentions.<br>• Assess impact of interventions on organizational culture.<br>• Find ways to continuously improve.<br>• Collect information and feed it back accurately and clearly. |

*Adapted from* ASTD Models for Human Performance Improvement *by William Rothwell, 1996.*

"Level 2 Evaluation"; No. 9815, "Level 3 Evaluation"; No. 9816, "Level 4 Evaluation"; and No. 9805, "Level 5 Evaluation: ROI"). As you read these *Info-line* issues, remember that you need to work with the parts of the models that focus on measuring results.

The output of the evaluation of results phase is a well-documented account of the changes that took place in the organization with an emphasis on the benefits achieved as a result of the HPI process.

## Basic HPI Competencies

Before leaping into the world of HPI, you may want to examine your own skill and knowledge level. William Rothwell in *ASTD Models for Human Performance Improvement* provides a detailed description of the roles, competencies, and outputs associated with the performance consultant. He begins by listing the core competencies associated with practitioners of HPI.

How do you rate yourself in relationship to these capabilities? From the following list, check the core competencies that you possess, and look for ways to improve in the areas that you feel you lack some capabilities.

- industry awareness
- leadership skills
- interpersonal relationship skills
- technological awareness and understanding
- problem-solving skills
- systems thinking and understanding
- performance and understanding
- knowledge of interventions
- business understanding
- organization understanding
- negotiating/contracting skills
- buy-in/advocacy skills
- coping skills
- ability to see "big picture"
- consulting skills

Rothwell also defines competencies for the separate roles effected by an HPI practitioner. Refer to the *HPI Process, Roles, and Skills* chart at left for a visual reference.

## Moving to Performance Improvement

Much has been written about the transition from training to HPI. *Webster's Dictionary* defines "transition" as the "passage from one place, condition, or stage to another." We all know that a caterpillar transitions to a butterfly and a tadpole transitions to a frog. The idea that training professionals need to "transition" to HPI professionals is both scary and misleading.

The misleading part of the transition is the thought that an increased need for HPI specialists will eliminate the need for skilled instructors. While it is certainly true that HPI is not about a new way of training employees, it is also true that an organization's need to train its employees will never be eliminated. It follows logically that the need for skilled instructors will never be eliminated. Think about it, did the growth in the need for skilled instructional designers eliminate the need for skilled instructors? The apprehensive part of the transition is the thought that to be an HPI specialist, you need to be an expert in all the possible interventions.

Again, look at the role of an instructional designer. A skilled instructional designer knows how to partner with SMEs to design and develop a training program for which he or she is not a content expert. HPI specialists also need to partner with experts within a specific discipline to implement appropriate interventions.

A better way to look at the movement towards HPI is as an "expansion." Again using *Webster's*, expansion is defined as the "act of increasing the range, scope, volume, size, etc. of." This means that we, as HPI specialists, need to be prepared to offer more than just a training solution in our efforts to help our clients improve their individual and organizational performance.

# References & Resources

## Articles

Carr, C., and L. Totzke. "The Long and Winding Path (from Instructional Technology to Performance Technology)." *Performance & Instruction,* August 1995, pp. 4-8.

Elliot, P. "Power-Charging People's Performance." *Training & Development,* December 1996, pp. 46-49.

Galagan, P. "Reinventing the Profession." *Training & Development,* December 1994, pp. 20-27.

Gephart, M.A. "The Road to High Performance," *Training & Development,* June 1995, pp. 30-38.

Gill, S.J. "Shifting Gears for High Performance." *Training & Development,* May 1995, pp. 24-31.

Harless, J. "Performance Technology Skills in Business: Implications for Preparation." *Performance Improvement Quarterly,* vol. 8, no. 4 (1995), pp. 75-88.

Rummler, G. "In Search of the Holy Performance Grail." *Training & Development,* April 1996, pp. 26-32.

Smalley, K., et al. "Strategic Planning: From Training to Performance Technology within Three Years." *Performance Improvement Quarterly,* vol. 8, no. 2 (1995), pp. 114-124.

Sorohan, E.G. "The Performance Consultant at Work," *Training & Development,* March 1996, pp. 35-38.

## Books

ASTD. *Introduction to Performance: A Primer for Trainers.* Alexandria, Virginia: ASTD, 1996.

Bassi, L.J., et al., *The ASTD Training Data Book.* Alexandria, Virginia: ASTD, 1996.

Browsher, J.E. *Revolutionizing Workforce Performance: A Systems Approach to Mastery.* San Francisco: Jossey-Bass Pfeiffer, 1998.

Dubois, D.D. *Competency-Based Performance Improvement.* Amherst, Massachusetts: HRD Press, 1995.

French, Wendell, and Cecil Bell. *Organizational Development: Behavioral Science Interventions for Organization Improvement.* New York: Prentice Hall, 1994.

Gilbert, T.F. *Human Competence Engineering Worthy Performance.* New York: McGraw-Hill, 1978.

Harbour, J.L. *The Basics of Performance Measurement.* New York: Quality Resources, 1997.

Kaufman, R. *Strategic Planning: An Organizational Guide (revised edition).* Newbury Park, California: Sage Publications, 1992.

Kaufman, R., et al. *The Practitioner's Handbook on Organization and Human Performance Improvement.* San Diego, California: University Associates/Pfeiffer, 1995.

Kirkpatrick, D.L. *Evaluating Training Programs: The Four Levels.* San Francisco: Berrett-Koehler, 1994.

Robinson, D.G., and J.C. Robinson. *Performance Consulting.* San Francisco: Berrett-Koehler, 1995.

Rothwell W. *ASTD Models for Human Performance Improvement.* Alexandria, Virginia: ASTD, 1996.

———. *Beyond Training and Development: State-of-the-Art Strategies for Enhancing Human Performance.* New York: AMACOM, 1996.

# References & Resources

Rummler, G., and A. Brache. *Improving Performance: How to Manage the White Space on the Organization Chart.* San Francisco: Jossey-Bass, 1995.

Smith, Martin (ed.) *Introduction to Performance Technology.* International Society for Performance Improvement, 1986.

Stolovitch, Harold D., and Erica J. Keeps. *Handbook of Human Performance Technology: A Comprehensive Guide for Analyzing and Solving Performance Problems in Organizations.* San Francisco: Jossey-Bass, 1992.

Swanson, R.A. *Analysis for Improving Performance: Tools for Diagnosing Organizations & Documenting Workplace Expertise.* San Francisco: Jossey-Bass, 1992.

## *Info-lines*

"Be a Better Needs Analyst." No. 8502 (revised 1998).

Bricker, B. "Basics of Performance Technology." No. 9211.

Carr, D.A. "How to Facilitate." No. 9406.

Callahan, M. "From Training to Performance Consulting." No. 9702.

———. "The Role of the Performance Intervention Specialist." No. 9714.

Kirrane, Diane. "The Role of the Performance Needs Analyst." No. 9713.

Koehle, Deborah. "The Role of the Performance Change Manager." No. 9715.

Gill, S. "Linking Training to Performance Goals." No. 9606 (revised 1998).

Sparhawk, Sally, and Marian Schickling. "Strategic Needs Analysis." No. 9408.

**Job Aid**

# HPI Process Checklist

Use this checklist as you advance through the phases of the performance improvement process.

## Phase 1: Conduct a Performance Analysis

**Technique:** Use a variety of methods (such as interviews, focus groups, and surveys) to determine the performance gap. Answer the following questions:

☐ What is the desired performance verses what is actually happening?

☐ What is the difference (gap) in performance?

☐ Who is affected?

☐ What is the impact?

**Output:** A clearly defined problem or opportunity, complete with conditions that surround the performance and concrete measurements that can be used in the evaluation phase.

## Phase 2: Conduct a Cause Analysis

**Technique:** Use a variety of methods (such as a fishbone diagram) to determine why the performance gap exists. Consider all of the causes that may apply, such as the following:

| | | |
|---|---|---|
| ☐ knowledge | ☐ motivation | ☐ rewards |
| ☐ skills | ☐ expectations | ☐ incentives |
| ☐ tools | ☐ performer's ability | ☐ consequences |
| ☐ environmental support | ☐ feedback | ☐ results |

**Output:** A clearly defined list of causes that includes the target group involved.

## Phase 3: Select, Design, and Develop Interventions

**Technique:** Use the following guideline to help determine intervention requirements.

☐ What results should be seen?

☐ What is important to stakeholders?

☐ What are limitations to budget, time, and resources?

☐ Brainstorm possible interventions and then choose appropriate interventions based on benefits and advantages verses costs and disadvantages.

Hint: More than one intervention may be required to establish and maintain correct performance while extinguishing incorrect performance.

☐ Create a project plan that includes major tasks, resources required, and timing/dates for each intervention.

☐ Develop a pilot intervention and test it, prior to producing the final intervention.

**Output:** A selection/design document that includes intervention components, major tasks, resources required, and timing. A development project plan that indicates development dates, pilot tests, and revision time.

## Phase 4: Implement the Intervention

**Technique:** Use the following strategy to implement an intervention that affects the four parts of the implementation phase: intervention, organization, leadership, and individuals.

☐ Gather implementation team and gain support from the intervention sponsor.

☐ Determine implementation strategy.

☐ Prepare the implementation team, target group, and organization by clarifying expectations.

☐ Identify possible intervention implementation weaknesses (such as those listed below) and create strategies to address the weaknesses.

- The intervention is hard to learn.
- The external workload increased.
- Users were not involved in the process.

**Output:** An implemented intervention (such as a new computer system, reorganization, a new process, a training program, or an incentive system).

## Job Aid

### Phase 5: Manage Change

**Technique:** Using the statements below, identify how people are reacting to the change, and address those reactions.

☐ Identify the target group's change stages.

☐ Determine strategy to address change states:

- Be a spokesperson for the intervention or change.
- Provide clear, reliable information about the intervention or change.
- Provide incentives or rewards.

**Output:** An on-going status report (often newsletter articles, videos, or peer discussions) of how well the intervention is working, the effect on the target group, and modifications made.

_____

_____

_____

### Phase 6: Evaluate the Results

**Technique:** Use the following strategy to evaluate how well the intervention met its desired outcome.

☐ Reaction: Use an intervention satisfaction survey.

☐ Learning: Use assessments, interviews, focus groups, or surveys to determine if "they got it."

☐ Behavior: Use observations, interviews, focus groups, or surveys to determine if the performance gap no longer exists.

☐ Results: Use observations, interviews, documents, or surveys to determine if the impact of the performance gap no longer exists.

**Output:** A report of the measurable changes taking place in the organization with an emphasis on the benefits associated with the HPI process.

_____

_____

_____

# From Training to
# Performance Consulting

Issue 9702

# From Training to Performance Consulting

**AUTHOR:**

**Madelyn Callahan**

**Editor**
Cat Sharpe

**Associate Editor**
Patrick McHugh

**Designer**
Steven M. Blackwood

**Copy Editor**
Leanne Eline

**ASTD Internal Consultant**
Michele Brock

# Resolution for Change

*"A paradigm shift is underway in the training field that requires training professionals to shift their focus from such traditional development inputs as classes and hours to such outputs as performance at the individual, team, and organizational levels. . . . The shift from training to performance is beginning to manifest itself in changing titles, perceptions, and skill requirements for trainers."*

—William J. Rothwell

To many, the shift from training to performance consulting means learning a new language. Trainees or learners become performers, trainers become performance consultants. The training department becomes a performance consulting center, performance improvement department, or performance enhancement division. Training needs become performance needs; training problems, performance problems; and training goals, performance goals.

Attempting this change involves more than just semantics. Make no mistake, the transition from training to performance consulting is an ambitious undertaking for any organization. What may appear on the surface to be a simple switch in terms and titles may actually require a complete reworking of the training department's philosophy and purpose.

Just what is behind this emphasis on performance? For several years, researchers, human resource and organizational development experts, business specialists, companies, and even trainers themselves have encountered situations where time and again training has not always been the only—or the best—solution to an organization's problems.

The ongoing discovery is that companies need to improve performance just to stay competitive in the increasingly complex global marketplace. To that end, every facet of the organization—each work function and operation—must change its focus to performance. It has also been determined that the best actions for improving performance typically involve nontraining interventions such as reorganizing key business operations or creating new product development processes. In cases where training solutions are appropriate, the emphasis on improving performance is directly linked to meeting specific organizational needs or goals.

Before the shift from training to performance improvement, a line manager seeking to boost production volume or quality might select a new technology and ask the training department to instruct employees to use the new process or equipment. The training department would respond by designing and delivering training according to management's specifications.

An organization's performance consulting department, however, would respond to a manager's initial request with either a multilevel or mini needs assessment followed by a presentation of the results and corresponding recommendations for solving any performance problems or opportunities for improvement. Key features of the consultants' work would be the clear and deliberate linking of performance needs and goals with organizational needs and goals.

Many practitioners find that a key step to the achievement of performance improvement involves applying the principles of human performance technology or HPT. HPT is defined as a systemic process that links business strategy and goals with a variety of interventions, which may or may not include training. This process includes performance analysis, cause analysis, and the selection of appropriate interventions.

This issue of *Info-line* will provide trainers with the guidance and resources necessary to reinvent training departments into performance consulting departments. It will describe the HPT process and the steps you can take to make a smooth, effective transition. It also outlines the responsibilities, duties, and competencies expected of new performance consultants.

## Not So Fast: Make Changes Gradually

A word to the wise is to plan your transition carefully and avoid making changes all at once. Sometimes pushing gives the transition project a quick-change feel that raises flags for managers and employees alike. If your traditional training department has been fairly active, consider a slower approach to phasing it out and replacing it with a performance improvement center.

Here are some steps to take in the slow lane:

1. Begin the phase-out process by acquainting employees with the new performance function—set up a consulting center, office, or department as part of the training department.

2. Start with a core group of two full-time and up to four part-time consultants.

3. Expect part-time staff to devote half their time to the new consulting services and the other half to providing training.

4. If the department has more training to complete than new consulting, expect to direct part-time consulting staff to focus on more demanding training projects already underway.

Find out details. Scan the organization's documents and resources, observe operations, and talk to people to find out past problems, future goals, and current obstacles to achieving those goals or overcoming problems. Proceed as follows:

● Carefully define the function's mission, services, goals, and scope of activity.

● Make this information public and be sure to let employees and managers know how the new function will benefit them.

● Talk to key decision makers to be sure you have their support for the change and to secure their commitment of resources or assistance to make this transition successful.

● Track your progress and results.

Once you achieve success, make sure everyone knows. Learn from your mistakes so you won't repeat them. Some obvious problems to avoid are:

● Costly projects, lack of client commitment, or those projects requiring little expertise.

● Projects that do not yield measurable results.

● Projects with interventions that have already been planned by the client.

## Transition

The true value of training to your organization could well determine a transition from a focus on training to one on performance improvement. For too long, too many companies and too many human resource and development or training departments have relied on training solutions to combat or solve every obstacle or problem the business faced. Worse yet, many of these costly training interventions were not directly tied to a specific business need or goal.

When companies begin to wonder about the efficacy of across-the-board training applications, they should ask the following four questions of every training intervention:

1. Is training the solution? It's important to find out if training is the best answer to a problem, if it is the entire answer, or just part of the answer.

2. Will training in this particular area provide the biggest return on investment (ROI)? If the costs to deliver training are high, will the value of the expected result at least match those costs?

3. Is the focus performance improvement? Should the training then be assessed according to its effect on performance?

4. Can training solve the problem on its own, or are other types of actions needed? Do other aspects of performance—such as improving feedback about performance, specifying job expectations, and establishing job support features and resources—need to be addressed?

### Altering Your Thoughts and Actions

Your first step toward making the transition is to change your own mindset. Individual perceptions affect the way you work and the actions you take. So before you begin making or recommending department-wide reforms, focus on changing your personal work habits and attitudes by attending to the following tasks:

**Concentrate on performance.** Think through your commitment to improving performance as your key contribution to the organization.

**Delve into self-directed study.** Read as many seminal works on the subject, by experts in the field such as Peter Block, Dana Gaines Robinson, James Robinson, Geary Rummler, Joe Harless, Tom Gilbert, Peter Pike, and Robert Mager. (See the "References & Resources" section at the end of this *Info-line* for some suggested reading.)

**Increase your formal education.** Take some graduate-level courses in finance, sales, marketing, HPT, and organizational development. Make sure you also acquire basic skills in sampling, surveying and gathering, as well as using statistical research.

**Upgrade your own competencies.** Concentrate on areas such as training technologies, on-the-job training (OJT), job and task analysis, combining learning with actual job functions, and identifying and working with subject matter experts.

**Develop professional networks.** Find other people who work with human performance technology. Professional associations and other groups offer you the opportunity to communicate and share knowledge with your peers.

**Immerse yourself in the business.** In other words, if your company designs software, either become a software designer—or learn what is required to be a software designer and know the day-to-day responsibilities of that position; this way you are conversant and knowledgeable on the subject. Find out about the kind of performance improvements that are needed, and gain experience on the job and in the work environment. If necessary, work side by side with line managers or volunteer your time on the line or in work teams.

**Talk to expert coaches.** External consultants can help you acquire the knowledge and skills you may need to guide your department through the transition to performance improvement, to coach your staff of performance consultants, or to create a performance model and strategic plan specifically designed for your department.

## Designing a Performance Consulting Center

The change to a focus on performance affects every aspect of your training department. Here are some provinces and duties that can typically change when a training department assumes the complete role of performance consulting center.

### ■ *Mission*
The training department's mission is to determine the learning needs of employees and deliver training to fulfill those needs. The performance improvement function is to determine the performance needs of employees and to deliver the best solution to fulfill those needs.

### ■ *Interactions with Managers*
Training departments traditionally assist managers by responding to their requests for training. Often, managers ask for specific training projects and the trainers deliver those programs accordingly. Performance consulting offers managers expertise in the area of needs assessment and problem diagnosis. Performance consultants make recommendations to managers based on research and observation.

### ■ *Needs Assessment*
Training needs assessment can identify the subject areas that employees may want or need to learn about. Performance assessment identifies performance gaps between actual and desired performance, and the problems or needs causing the gaps. It also identifies workplace challenges or obstacles to achieving desired performance. For additional information on conducting needs assessments, see *Info-line* No. 8502, "Be a Better Needs Analyst"; No. 9408, "Strategic Needs Analysis"; and No. 9611, "Conducting a Mini Needs Assessment."

### ■ *Measuring Results*
Training evaluation measures only learning and involves a survey of impressions and responses from the participant. Performance evaluation uses employee responses to measure how much employees have learned, but it also measures changes in performance and whether employees are able to transfer learning and new skills to their jobs. Cost-benefit analysis is also used to measure the effectiveness of the interventions. To learn how to conduct a cost-benefit analysis, refer to *Info-line* No. 9007, "How to Conduct a Cost-Benefit Analysis."

### ■ *Focus*

Training departments maintain a narrow focus on learning and on the products of the learning function, which include computer-based, self-paced, and other structured training programs. If learning objectives are achieved, the trainer's job is complete. Performance consulting must effect changes and help improve performance—which may include providing some training. But it also involves providing guidance to achieve desired performance goals that link directly to stated business goals. Consultants must also help performers overcome any barriers to desired performance. If performance improves, performance consultants have fulfilled their role.

### ■ *Training as an Investment*

Most organizations see training as a cost—instead of an investment—and rarely acknowledge any link between training efforts and business goals. Performance improvement projects and interventions produce results that can be measured in terms of cost, increased productivity, higher sales, or quality improvements—results directly linked to business needs and goals.

### ■ *Accountability*

For training departments, accountability is measured in terms of department activity, such as the number of instructor and participant days, as well as the number of courses. The performance department is held accountable for its effect on operations throughout the company and for its ability to build and maintain partnerships with decision makers and management at all organizational levels. The department must answer for the state of training quality, performance improvement, and contributions to operational outcomes.

## Easing the Transition

Here are some suggestions from trainers who've made the transition to performance consulting within their own organizations. The key is to start with minimal changes. One of the least disruptive changes you can make is to rename the training or human resources department to focus attention on performance improvement, innovation, or enhancement. Then, follow-up with other, more substantive modifications.

- Change titles—for example, from human resources specialists or training specialists to performance specialists or performance consultants.

- Review all department functions. Add or eliminate services to recast your efforts in line with specific performance improvement goals.

- Record these changes in a newly formulated mission statement.

- Communicate with line managers often; inform and educate them about your goals and ideas for the new department in addition to marketing the new function internally.

- Introduce your department—and gain consulting work—by doing a workshop for line managers on how performance improvement differs from strictly *training* workers.

Continue to perform those functions, such as meetings facilitation, that may not have a direct effect on performance, but will help to prepare the work environment and the workforce for positive changes in performance. Expect to have to earn the respect and credibility of line managers, don't simply expect them to bring their business to you. Additionally, honor managers' requests: if you're asked to deliver training even though you're sure it's not the best solution, go ahead and fulfill the request—but do your own needs assessment and use the results when you present that manager with specific proposals for consulting assistance.

## Key Competencies For Success

### Skill Areas Include:

**Building relationships.** Be able to develop business relationships and professional networks covering a wide variety of groups and individuals.

**Coaching.** Be able to help others identify and comprehend such personnel issues as needs, values, problems, options, and goals.

**Collaborating.** Be able to work effectively with others as partners both in and out of the department.

**Facilitating group processes.** Be able to interact with and influence groups to help them deal with job tasks, business relationships and interactions, and the needs of individuals.

**Managing projects.** Be able to lead or influence others in positive ways and to plan, organize, track, and monitor progress on complex work assignments.

**Observing performance.** Be able to monitor and provide detailed descriptions of job behaviors and of the outcome of those behaviors.

**Providing feedback.** Be able to clearly communicate information, ideas, assessments, suggestions, observations, and conclusions for the purpose of helping others to understand and act on problems.

**Questioning.** Be able to gather data and information by a variety of means, including interviews, questionnaires, and observation.

**Reviewing data and drawing conclusions.** Be able to scan, synthesize, and summarize information; then be able to use the information to make deductions about a situation or problem.

### Knowledge Areas Include:

**Business.** Be familiar with the ways businesses operate and how particular business functions work together to move company operations along.

**Economics.** Understand how business decisions have a direct effect on work results and on the economic well-being of the company.

**Self-knowledge.** Know and understand your own personal needs, values, interests, work style, and professional competencies—and understand how these personal attributes affect those around you.

**Interventions.** Understand the various ways performance can be improved in organizations and know how to apply particular interventions to close gaps between real and desired performance.

### Developing New Training Roles

Professionals at every level of the HRD/training department who are seeking to reinvent their roles will need to take some proactive steps to effect these changes. Following is a description of some traditional training and HRD roles and how the transition in each role will begin to encompass the new objectives of a performance consulting function.

#### ■ Training and HRD Directors

These positions must take the lead in moving toward performance improvement. If the people in these roles say "Yes," they are responsible for and must set out to educate and inform their clients about this change. They must safeguard the processes and skills necessary to take on a performance focus. They must also take the helm, directing and managing others to complete the transition.

#### ■ Training Analysts and Designers

Analysts and designers must possess the right skills to zero in on each training request and identify the precise performance issues that need to be addressed if employees are to succeed at their jobs and if the organization is to realize the value of its investment.

#### ■ Training Developers

These course developers must design reality-based exercises. In order to do this they must have enough information about the actual work environment and about the actual performance system currently in place to build effective performance improvement programs.

#### ■ Training Instructors

These instructors must also understand the actual human performance system that the employees experience, so they'll comprehend employees' questions and concerns.

# Performance Roles

There are four main roles that performance consultants must assume as they maintain their primary focus on improving employee performance. These roles are:

1. Performance analyst.

2. Intervention specialist.

3. Change manager.

4. Performance evaluator.

The performance analyst functions as a troubleshooter who identifies gaps between actual and desired performance and targets specific performance areas for improvement; the intervention specialist picks the best interventions to close the performance gaps; the change manager makes sure that interventions are conducted in the most efficient ways for helping performers achieve goals; and the performance evaluator measures the effect of interventions and continues to monitor the long-term impact of these changes.

## Competencies

In staffing a new performance-centered department, it's important to establish exactly what the performance consultants will be expected to know and do. Among the various performance models used to derive this information, certain skills and knowledge areas remain standard for filling out the role of the performance consultant. It's up to each consultant to develop competency in these areas.

According to Dana Gaines Robinson, president of Pittsburgh, Pennsylvania-based Partners in Change and co-author of *Performance Consulting*, performance consultants need to know about human performance technology, but they also need more than knowledge. Here is a collection of core competencies gathered from Robinson's work and from the book *ASTD Models for Human Performance Improvement* by William J. Rothwell.

**Systems thinking.** This involves being able to assess a performance problem and performance intervention in terms of the big picture. It's important to see how all business functions are integrated, how they affect the operations, needs, and goals of the organization, and how performance problems and interventions affect the organization overall.

**Business acumen.** This provides the background you need to understand the client organization in financial terms—in other words, how the business makes money. You must be able to read and understand financial reports, annual reports, operating statements, and so forth. With this knowledge you'll be able to talk to line managers and earn their trust by demonstrating in-depth understanding of the business and of the inner workings of business functions.

**Industry awareness.** This involves an overarching understanding of the vision, strategy, goals, and culture of the particular industry to which your client organization belongs.

**Analytical and diagnostic skills.** The specific abilities you need to measure the performance gap are to:

- sample populations

- construct a reliable survey

- interview people, observe and assess performance on the job

- gather, evaluate, and present information

**Collaborative consulting skills.** These skills enable you to form partnerships and influence others throughout every level of the organization.

**Interviewing skills.** These skills are needed in order to help clients discover what their real needs are, to let go of or change deep-rooted assumptions about their needs and problems, and to decide on an action to improve performance.

**Negotiating and contracting skills.** These skills enable you to organize, prepare, manage, and evaluate proposals, agreements, and final work from vendors, external consultants, outsourcing agents, and others working outside the organization.

## Basic Consulting Skills

Following are a few basic skills you need to be an effective performance consultant. If you feel you don't have these skills, start thinking about ways you can develop them. To be a successful performance consultant you must:

- plan and conduct needs assessment surveys and interviews; analyze the results

- facilitate interviews and consensus gathering

- analyze organizational structures, operations, and integrated work functions

- use flow charts to diagram or map out work operations and processes

- prepare statements of work standards and work expectations

- write action plans and performance contracts

- work with various technologies including performance support systems

- facilitate change by conducting interventions

- pick out evaluation tools or design them to measure the various procedures and products your department produces

- be familiar with employee appraisal practices and programs

- compile and present reports on data and recommendations resulting from the interventions

### Responsibilities of Performance Consultants

In general, trainers who will succeed as performance consultants and who will implement the improved performance required by organizations will be expected to do the following:

- Build cooperative business relationships with important decision makers, managers, and other key associates.

- Possess a thorough understanding of the goals, vision, and strategies that the organization's leaders are trying to accomplish.

## Effective Consulting Through Collaboration

For trainers making the transition to performance consulting, the best approach to consulting involves collaboration between consultant and client. This capitalizes on both the consultant's training and HR expertise and the client's detailed knowledge of the business operation, political access, and ability to generate staff support. This approach requires that both sides share decision making and plans for taking action.

Here's why this collaborative consulting style is a winner:

- Problem assessment and diagnosis tend to be on target because contributions of ideas and information are solicited from both the client and the consultant.

- While this process takes more time to develop and implement, the client and consultant can save time in the long run by "doing it right the first time."

- As a decision-making partner, the client is more apt to understand and support those decisions rather than resisting them.

- There is a high likelihood that the desired outcome will result because both the consultant and the client take all the actions that have been determined.

- Throughout the planning and execution of this process, both client and consultant learn more about the business and about specific challenges to performance improvement—and they are able to put that learning to use for later efforts.

- Throughout the process, the client and consultant forge a new, stronger relationship as they develop trust and respect that will allow them to work more productively together in the future.

- Determine the level of performance that employees must achieve to improve the organization's well-being.

- Identify needed changes in the workplace for performance improvement to take place.

- Consult with managers and others to define every action for achieving high performance.

## Performance Consultants as Business Professionals

Performance consultants with a training background are knowledgeable, skilled professionals who are also keen businesspeople willing to immerse themselves in the details of their client's business. What's more, these consultants approach their specialty, human performance, with the same business acumen as their colleagues specializing in finance, marketing, or operations. Performance consultants should be able to:

- Review and comprehend in detail the organization's annual report.

- Participate in discussions with management about ways to measure and compare current performance levels against organizational goals and identify actions to achieve goals.

- Determine what forces beyond the organization's control may make it difficult for the organization to achieve its goals.

- Research and discuss the effect of competitors' strategies and their actions as they affect you or your client's organization.

- Speak the organization's language; be comfortable using terms commonly understood throughout the organization.

- Stay up-to-date on professional journals, magazines, and government reports as expected of management staff working within the organization.

- Be familiar with the organization's own collection of documents such as mission statements, sales and marketing plans, annual reports, operations reports, new product development plans, customer service surveys, etc.

- Agree to work on a group project designed to handle a specific aspect of the business such as human resources, marketing, quality, or customer service—and in the process learn about colleagues' concerns.

- Take time off from your consultant's role and pursue special projects for several months to gain critical information and insight into the manufacturing, customer service, or maintenance operations of your client organization.

- Closely observe the top performers in the organization; work with them in a partnership for several days and ask questions about the strategies they use to achieve goals and the obstacles they must confront.

## Guiding Departmental Change

To reinvent the training department, begin by refocusing the department's mission statement to emphasize performance. Next, redefine the departmental goals to fit the new focus. Finally, establish selection criteria for accepting projects.

### Writing a New Mission Statement

The mission statement must give the organization a synopsis of the department's objectives and the kinds of services the department will provide. A mission statement must tell the organization:

1. The performance consultants on your staff will work with line managers and share the responsibility for performance improvement projects.

2. The consultants will pick performance improvement initiatives that are aligned with business goals and needs as well as with line managers' or other clients' requests.

3. The consultants will focus primarily on improving employee performance and will recommend various methods for improvement, including electronic performance support systems.

4. The consultants will deliver the needed interventions or direct internal clients to consultants or providers outside the organization.

## Year One: Clearly Defined Goals

Specify the goals your department intends to achieve in its first year. For example, within your first 12 months you may want to complete the following tasks:

- Conduct an organizational review or scan of various aspects such as the business operations, culture, management practices, processes, physical work environment, and barriers to progress.

- Select a number of projects you know are likely to succeed.

- Finish several of the projects and conduct an in-depth evaluation of each one.

- Put together and execute a plan to market the consulting function.

- Identify intervention sources both inside and outside the organization.

## Fine-tune Your Scope with Parameters

To determine the scope of your projects, set limitations or specifications for the kinds of projects you're willing to accept. Selection criteria may include such features as:

- three-month deadlines
- links to business goals
- client ownership
- funding

No project can extend beyond three months during the first year. The idea is to produce fast, powerful results to put before the organization's leadership. Each project must link to specific business goals and needs so that the effectiveness of the interventions can be measured and the results demonstrated. This information will help consultants change and adjust the interventions to improve their success rate, and it should be clear that both the client and the consulting staff share a stake in the success of the project and share responsibility for that project. The company must also commit financial resources and support for operating the consulting service and funding the interventions.

## Preparing Your Training Staff

Once you've established your specifications for accepting projects, it's time to begin building your staff and getting your trainers ready for their new jobs as consultants. Remember that this is one of the most difficult parts of the transition to refocusing your department on performance consulting. Proceed with caution and, above all, patience.

Here are a few suggestions for implementing changes to your staff: Begin developing your staff by reviewing the differences between the training role and the performance consulting role. Go through your list of staff members and decide which ones have the skills to be effective consultants. If you don't have anyone with the required skills, start searching outside the department. To facilitate your search, put together a list of the abilities and duties that are linked to the consulting function's mission and goal statements.

If you have one staff member with experience in consulting, you can pair that person with someone else on staff who may have just a few basic consulting skills. If experienced in performance consulting, this partnership may act as your core consulting team. The trick here is to find people with enough experience and skill between them to make the partnership effective.

Take the time and make the effort to prepare your staff sufficiently so that you're debuting this consulting department with a staff that is reasonably experienced. That may mean having to bring in external consultants to assist with the first few interventions. This would help you gain the trust and credibility of the organization and it would be a skill-building opportunity for your staff.

## Conducting an Organizational Scan

Take a month to meet with key leaders and decision makers in the organization to find out how they define the primary business issues. This is crucial information for selecting projects that have a high potential for securing management support, providing results you can measure, and producing performance improvement. Plus, once you've collected all the data and information you need from these interviews, you'll be able to finalize your department's goals so that they're closely linked with the organization's overall business plans, needs, and goals.

As you conduct your organizational scan, top-level managers should give you clear answers regarding:

- one- to five-year all-encompassing goals for the organization

- the most important issues behind each department's activities, efforts, and achievements

- the effect of new technology on the organization's economic well-being and future goals

- 12-month goals for each department

- potential opportunities and challenges for the organization

- the main clients in departments singled out for projects

- ways to assess client satisfaction in targeted departments

- business links in these departments

- negatives and positives associated with these departments over the past several years

## Meeting the Managers

A common mistake of fledgling performance consulting departments is to leave the initial projects to chance. In addition to bringing in external help if it's needed, there are a few precautions you can take to guard against disaster. First, pick projects you've researched and found are very likely to succeed, then arrange meetings with decision makers and line managers who have an interest in these projects and use the meeting to present the projects and sell your services.

As you discuss the projects, refer to the results of your audits and assessments and point out the long- and short-term problems these managers may be experiencing. Explain clearly and succinctly how your consulting services may help alleviate some of their problems. Try to generate interest and enthusiasm, but do not raise unrealistic expectations. Finally, go over the parameters of the projects and be sure that all agree on project goals and on precisely how the projects' successes will be measured.

## Developing Your Products and Services

Once you've completed your organizational scan and established your goals for the new department, you're ready to begin planning and putting together your products and services for the new consulting department. Keep in mind that as you formulate your department's offerings to the organization, you are making decisions about selling your department to potential internal clients. That is, the products and services you offer must be relevant and useful to your organization.

Examples of products and services include:

- structured performance audits to determine current levels of job performance

- evaluation and assessment tools that measure training and performance interventions

- analyses of organizational maps

- performance contracts

- effects of performance improvement strategies on organizational plans, business operations, work procedures, and individual performance

- programs for team building

- assessment procedures for evaluating client satisfaction and product quality

## Performance Improvement and HPT

The performance improvement process involves applying human performance technology. Experts offer a variety of models for putting Human Performance Technology (HPT) into practice, but all share these key steps:

1. Identify business needs linked to performance gaps, which are based on a formal assessment.

2. Establish desired performance goals that can be measured—and that link directly to organizational goals.

3. Decide on the type and level of performance needed to accomplish those goals.

4. Determine potential obstacles to attaining desired performance.

5. Identify the best solutions and performance interventions that can be used to remove or overcome those obstacles and to close the gap between real and ideal performance.

6. Conduct an evaluation to make sure those goals have been reached and the performance gaps have been closed.

The basic parts of the process include:

■ *Performance Analysis*
Measure the performance gap between the actual and desired performance to identify performance problems and opportunities for performance improvement. The first needs assessment identifies competencies and abilities workers must have to produce the desired performance and achieve organizational goals. A second assessment measures the workers' current skills and abilities, organizational effectiveness, and the organization's position against competitors.

Performance analysts rely on a variety of resources to conduct assessments, including background information on the organization as well as interviews with focus groups, subject matter experts, customers, suppliers, employees, senior management, line managers, and supervisors.

## Case Study: Delayed Development

The electric business unit of a major midwestern utility company faced the challenge of preparing employees for a more competitive, deregulated market environment. The utility initiated several projects for improving internal processes, including customer service.

One customer service initiative involved combining job roles: Customer service workers would have broader responsibilities instead of being specialists in one area. The aim was to provide a single point of contact for residential, commercial, and industrial customers.

The training department had to quickly design and develop cost-effective training for more than 200 employees in marketing and technical training so that they could become competent in their new roles in a short time. In the past, such development had occurred experientially, taking 10 to 15 years on average for an employee to reach the desired level of skills and knowledge.

The human performance analysis clearly defined the new work systems and new job roles. That enabled the utility to ensure that employees received the appropriate training for performing in the context of the changes. The training relied heavily on job aids and other performance-support tools, which lowered the training curve, cut the cost of reskilling employees, enabling employees to become productive and work safely in quick order.

The key to the training's success was its focus on organizational goals—such as creating a single point of contact for customers—and its focus on the outputs for meeting those goals. The overall effect was to move the company to a just-in-time, need-to-know approach to employee development.

The results include improved competence and confidence among employees, as well as better customer service and customer satisfaction. Employee productivity also rose due to less need for classroom training and more reliance on job aids and performance support. And employees reported greater job satisfaction with their broader job responsibilities.

"This analytical approach to employee development, which utilizes performance technologies, links specific training interventions to desired employee outputs, and it better targets training dollars," says a senior manager with the utility. "It is the key to focusing on the development of competencies related to increased responsiveness to our customers and our company's success in the competitive environment."

*Adapted from P. Elliott, "Power-Charging People's Performance,"*
Training & Development, *September 1995.*

# Case Study: Going Over Budget

A performance technologist received a request that said, "Teach our department managers how to keep costs within budget."

During the initial meeting with the client, a large manufacturing company, the technologist learned that managers routinely exceeded their budgets by 7 to 23 percent annually—and that the managers prepared their budgets without help and then submitted them to their vice presidents. Then the VPs and managers met to negotiate the budgets, which usually meant reducing the amount for many items.

A human performance analysis revealed that most of the managers that were unable to stay within their budgets didn't use the same skills and techniques to create their budgets as did the managers that stayed within budget. The budget-deficit managers also didn't use the same skills and techniques as their more successful counterparts to justify their numbers in negotiations with the VPs.

The analysis also revealed these facts:

- When managers overspent their budgets, they were "rewarded" by having their moneys increased the next year.

- Generally, new managers kept within or below their budgets the first two years. But after that, they exceeded their budgets.

- Many of the budget-deficit managers didn't know how to estimate costs accurately.

One solution was to give mangers training on projecting costs and preparing a budget based on those costs. They also received training in how to justify their numbers to VPs. In addition, the company established a policy that overspending would affect managers' performance evaluations negatively.

Managers could also request technical assistance from the financial department during budget preparation. And monthly reports were adjusted to show actual-versus-projected spending on each line item.

*Adapted from Paul Elliott, "Power-Charging People's Performance,"* Training & Development, *September 1995.*

■ *Cause Analysis*

Identify the underlying causes of a past, present, or potential performance gap. To discover the causes, consultants may survey performers to find out if performers understand the impact of their work on achieving organizational goals; if proper awards and incentives are in place to encourage high performance; if performers receive the right support in the form of data, information, resources, tools, job aids, working conditions, sufficient time, and feedback from managers and supervisors; if they receive support on a timely basis; and if they have the skills and knowledge they need to meet performance requirements.

■ *Implementation*

Manage the changes carefully so that you can successfully implement your interventions. As you prepare to install an intervention, keep an eye on both changes taking place within your organization, and external changes that may affect implementation. To maintain organizational support, reiterate to performers, managers, and others the benefits of the intervention for helping the organization meet its goals and objectives. Be sure to select the best talent and resources for the implementation.

The implementation part of the process may involve having to deal with adversity and reluctance to the transition. The most challenging aspect of implementing solutions is helping others overcome resistance to change and accept the intervention.

■ *Evaluation*

Assess the effectiveness of the intervention for improving performance. To do this, talk to performers, management, and the company's customers and suppliers about their views of the interventions. Then look at whether the performers are working better by using the new skills, knowledge, resources, or tools supplied during the intervention. Focus on results to determine whether the intervention has closed the performance gap and contributed to fulfilling organizational goals.

■ *Intervention*

A crucial step in the performance improvement process is selecting and designing actions or interventions needed to close the performance gap. Interventions may address a wide array of issues such as employee/employer expectations, knowledge and skill levels, feedback and job support, available resources and technologies, and business processes and operations. They may respond to needs in the areas of business, performance, training, or the workplace. They may also concentrate on specific functions such as hiring, recruiting, and selecting personnel; providing job support resources such as training, job aids, and feedback; upgrading the work environment such as improved designs for work flow, equipment and other resources, and availability of information and data; or providing motivation in the form of incentives, goals, and rewards.

Interventions also may focus on the external environment; the organization's leadership, mission, and strategy; its culture and performance; and individual performance levels. It may also focus on systems, structure, management practices, organizational performance, and issues that affect individuals such as motivation, needs and values, skills, and performance.

Following are some how-to's for designing and implementing interventions:

- Make sure the intervention is carefully targeted to produce results that match the amount of time, effort, and resources the organization is investing.

- Have a complete understanding of the situation based on reliable data from performance and cause analyses so that the intervention will be appropriate.

- Search the organizational hierarchy to locate a sponsor willing to commit the largest amount of financial and organizational resources to the project.

- Select design teams for creating interventions. Use a variety of experts to be sure you cover the range of skills and knowledge needed to work on the various performance problems of individual employees and organizations.

- Instruct the design team to come up with the lowest-cost intervention that solves the performance problem. This may require using off-the-shelf designs or adapting existing designs that fulfill your requirements.

- Using the resources at hand, aim for a comprehensive, long-term intervention. To make sure it's long-lasting, integrate the intervention into the business culture and operations.

- Expect to revise and revise and revise. No design is perfect on the first draft. Be willing to keep testing and making changes to get the exact intervention you need.

## After the Intervention

In the aftermath of a project, you have an opportunity to collect some of the most valuable data of the process—data you can use to sell your services further or to learn valuable lessons from mistakes that may not be very costly now but likely will be later. As you deal with evaluations, marketing, and mistakes, collect information and data from line managers and decision makers working with the projects, so you'll have some guidelines for measuring customer satisfaction.

1. If you've had some successes, don't be shy about asking those satisfied line managers, or other internal clients, to be spokespeople for your consulting services.

2. Suggest the managers and others endorse your services by writing up a brief announcement or testimonial for the company newsletter.

3. When you make your next presentation, invite those managers and other internal customers to come along and offer their endorsement.

4. Encourage managers and decision makers to discuss with their colleagues the performance consulting center's products and services.

5. Conduct postmortem reviews of unsuccessful projects to find out if the project was, in fact, inappropriate for the targeted performance problem; to learn from your mistakes and avoid similar glitches in current projects; and to assess whether the consulting staff needs additional skills training.

# References & Resources

## Articles

Carr, C., and L. Totzke. "The Long and Winding Path (from Instructional Technology to Performance Technology)." *Performance & Instruction,* August 1995, pp. 4-8.

Clark, R.C. "Hang Up Your Training Hat." *Training & Development,* September 1994, pp. 61-65.

Galagan, P. "Reinventing the Profession." *Training & Development,* December 1994, pp. 20-27.

Galagan, P. "Think Performance: A Conversation With Gloria Gery." *Training & Development,* March 1994, pp. 47-51.

Gill, S.J. "Shifting Gears for High Performance." *Training & Development,* May 1995, pp. 24-31.

Gephart, M.A. "The Road to High Performance." *Training & Development,* June 1995, pp. 30-38.

Harless, J. "Performance Technology Skills in Business: Implications for Preparation." *Performance Improvement Quarterly,* 1995, pp. 75-88.

Nancy, C. "Performance-Linked Training." *Public Personnel Management,* Winter 1988, pp. 457-463.

Regalbuto, G.A. "Recovery from Occupational Schizophrenia." *Training & Development,* May 1991, pp. 79-86.

Retts, C. "From Hierarchy to High Performance." *Training & Development,* October 1995, pp. 31-33.

Rummler, G. "In Search of the Holy Performance Grail." *Training & Development,* April 1996, pp. 26-32.

Sorohan, E.G. "The Performance Consultant at Work." *Training & Development,* March 1995, pp. 35-38.

———. "How to Reengineer Training Functions for Time and Quality Gains." *Training Director's Forum Newsletter,* September 1994, pp. 1-3.

———. "What to Avoid When Shifting From Training to Performance Consulting." *Training Director's Forum Newsletter,* March 1996, pp. 1-3.

———. "The Future of Workplace Learning and Performance." *Training & Development,* May 1994, pp. 36-47.

———. "Trends That Will Influence Workplace Learning and Performance in the Next Five Years." *Training & Development,* May 1994, pp. 29-35.

## Books

ASTD. *Introduction to Performance: A Primer for Trainers.* Alexandria, Virginia: American Society for Training & Development, 1996.

ASTD. *The ASTD Training & Development Handbook. A Guide to Human Resource Development.* 4th edition. Robert L. Craig, (ed.). Alexandria, Virginia: American Society for Training & Development, 1996.

Bellman, G.M. *The Consultant's Calling: Bringing Who You Are to What You Do.* San Francisco: Jossey-Bass, 1990.

Block, P. *Flawless Consulting: A Guide to Getting Your Expertise Used.* San Diego, California: Pfeiffer, 1981.

Brache, A.P., and G.A. Rummler. *Improving Performance: Managing the White Space on the Organizational Chart.* San Francisco: Jossey-Bass, 1990.

Broad, M.L., and J. W. Newstrom. *Transfer of Training.* Reading, Massachusetts: Addison-Wesley, 1992.

Brown, Mark Graham, et al. *Rx For Business A Troubleshooting Guide for Building a High Performance Organization.* Chicago, Illinois: Irwin Professional Publishing, 1996.

Dean, P.J. *Performance Engineering at Work.* Batavia, Illinois: International Board of Standards for Training, Performance, and Instruction, 1994.

Dubois, D.D. *Competency-Based Performance Improvement.* Amherst, Massachusetts: HRD Press, 1995.

Gilbert, T.F. *Human Competence: Engineering Worthy Performance.* New York: McGraw-Hill, 1978.

*Handbook of Human Performance Technology.* Washington, DC: National Society for Performance and Instruction, 1992.

Kaufman, Roger. "Assessing Needs," *Introduction to Performance Technology.* Washington, DC: National Society for Performance and Instruction, 1992.

———. *Strategic Thinking. A Guide to Identifying and Solving Problems.* Alexandria, Virginia: American Society for Training & Development and the International Society for Performance Improvement, 1996.

Kaufman, Roger, et al. *The Practitioner's Handbook on Organization and Human Performance Improvement.* San Diego: University Associates/Pfeiffer and Company, 1995.

Langdon, D. *The New Language of Work.* Amherst, MA: HRD Press, 1995.

Mager, R.F., and P. Pipe. *Analyzing Performance Problems* (2d ed.). Belmont, California: David S. Lake, 1984.

McLagan, P. *Models for HRD Practice.* Alexandria, Virginia: American Society for Training & Development, 1989.

Odenwald, Sylvia B., and William G. Matheny. *Global Impact: Award Winning Performance Programs from Around the World.* Chicago, Illinois: Irwin Professional Publishing, 1996.

Pepitone, J. *Future Training: A Roadmap for Restructuring the Training Function.* Dallas, Texas: AddVantage Learning Press, 1995.

Robinson, D.G., and J.C. Robinson. *Performance Consulting: Moving Beyond Training.* San Francisco: Berret-Koehler, 1995.

Robinson, D.G., and J.C. Robinson. *Training for Impact: How to Link Training to Business Needs and Measure the Results.* San Francisco: Jossey-Bass, 1989.

Rothwell, W.J. *ASTD Models for Human Performance Improvement: Roles, Competencies, and Outputs.* Alexandria, Virginia: American Society for Training & Development, 1996.

Stolovitch, H.D., and E.J. Keeps. *Handbook of Human Performance Technology: A Comprehensive Guide for Analyzing and Solving Performance Problems in Organizations.* San Francisco: Jossey-Bass, 1992.

Swanson, Richard A. *Analysis for Improving Performance. Tools for Diagnosing Organizations & Documenting Workplace Expertise.* San Francisco: Berrett-Koehler Publishers, 1996.

## Info-lines

Austin, M. "Needs Assessment by Focus Group." No. 9401 (revised 1998).

Bricker, B. "Training Basics: Basics of Performance Technology." No. 9211 (out of print).

Callahan, M. (ed.). "Be a Better Needs Analyst." No. 8502 (revised 1998).

———. "How to Conduct a Cost-Benefit Analysis." No. 9007 (revised 1997).

O'Neill, M. "How to Focus a Training Evaluation." No. 9605 (out of print).

Robinson, D.G., and J.C. Robinson. "Measuring Affective and Behavioral Change." No. 9110 (revised 1997).

Robinson, D.G., and J.C. Robinson. "Tracking Operational Results." No. 9112.

Waagen, Alice. "Essentials for Evaluation." No. 9705.

———. "Task Analysis." No. 9808.

Younger, S.M. "Learning Organizations: The Trainer's Role." No. 9306 (out of print).

# Training to Performance Consulting Transition Planner

For a smooth transition from training to performance improvement, make a plan. Never make sudden changes. Be sure to work into your plan's time frame a transitional period that will cover a sufficient amount of time. Here's a model for your planning strategy.

**1.** What is your position in the training department? State your title and write a short description of your duties and responsibilities.

**2.** Why is the training department changing its focus to performance consulting? List up to three reasons and include a short explanation with each.

**3.** As a stakeholder, what prompted you to agree with the change or go along with it?

    **a.** How will you change your perceptions and behaviors to prepare for the role of performance consultant? List up to five examples for each.

    **Perceptions:** _____

_____

_____

_____

_____

    **Behaviors:** _____

_____

_____

_____

_____

    **b.** How would you compare your current responsibilities as a trainer with those expected of a performance consultant?

**4.** What do you perceive are the six major differences between training departments and performance consulting departments?

**5.** How do you define your training department's current purpose? How would you redefine it according to your preferences for the performance consulting center?

**6.** What will you do to effect change?

    **a.** Select a new name for the department:

    **b.** Select new titles for training department staff:

    **c.** List performance consulting competencies and abilities that staff should have:

**7.** Write a new mission statement for the department that takes into account the results of an organizational scan.

    **a.** Define your department's criteria and parameters for accepting performance consulting projects.

    **b.** Specify the products and services your department will provide.

**8.** List the department's new goals and objectives and include links to corporate goals and objectives.

    **a.** Describe corresponding steps to achieve the department's goals.

    **b.** List general guidelines for implementing these steps and any other guidelines for change.

    **c.** Describe both the internal and external barriers to change that you expect to encounter and for each describe ways you can overcome those obstacles. Refer to specific strategies for change management.

# The Role of the Performance
# Needs Analyst

Issue 9713

# The Role of the Performance Needs Analyst

**A U T H O R :**

Diane Kirrane
Kirrane & Company
5406 Connecticut Ave, N.W.
Suite 201
Washington, DC 20015
Tel.: 202/363-7761

**Editor**
Cat Sharpe

**Associate Editor**
Patrick McHugh

**Designer**
Steven M. Blackwood

**Copy Editor**
Kay Larson

**ASTD Internal Consultant**
Dr. Walter Gray

# Analyzing Human Performance

Looking for trouble—and opportunities—related to human performance in the workplace is the first step in human performance improvement (HPI). Analyzing problems and opportunities to discover their cause or causes often indicates how to preserve and enhance what works and how to correct, replace, or eliminate what does not.

Looking for solutions to fill current performance gaps and opportunities to improve existing, but only adequate, performance levels is an ongoing process throughout the duration of HPI. The analyst role, however, is key at the start. His or her job is to get at root causes and aim further efforts at the right targets. The other roles in the HPI process: the intervention specialist, change manager, and evaluator, bring the process full circle. Sometimes, one person fills all the HPI roles; other times, especially if fundamental or widespread organizational change is anticipated, using a team of role specialists is appropriate.

This *Info-line* recommends thorough analysis to avoid misdirected effort. Analysis also helps scale the use of resources to the impact or potential impact of the problem or opportunity. And, methodical analysis begins a sequence that moves toward improvement rather than bogging down in "analysis paralysis."

## Performance Technology and HPI

Today the trend is to use performance technology to achieve performance improvement. Performance technology involves the following:

- thinking, analyzing, and planning strategically, holistically, and systematically

- establishing performance improvement goals and objectives tied to the work organization's mission, goals, and objectives

- combining tools and successful approaches from many fields that contribute information about how to improve performance

- considering how actions and interventions will add value to an organization and promote the achievement of its mission, goals, and objectives

- keeping customers in mind

- being proactive by forecasting needs as well as reacting to current needs

Many training and development professionals are building on their expertise to expand into performance consulting for HPI. These trainers are becoming knowledgeable about the range of factors that affect human performance at work. HPI is known by different monikers—human performance enhancement, human performance engineering, performance improvement—but, under whatever title, HPI involves the following elements:

- recognizing and analyzing current and future gaps between actual human performance and desired or optimal performance

- removing any barriers to desired or optimal performance

- designing, developing, and implementing cost-effective, ethical interventions that close performance gaps

- evaluating results using appropriate financial and nonfinancial measures, some of which (customer good will, for example) are intangible

# The HPI Analyst Role

The most important human performance improvement role is that of analyst. So, an analyst needs many skills. Listed below are the core competencies all HPI practitioners require:

- industry awareness
- leadership skills
- interpersonal skills
- technological awareness and understanding
- problem-solving skills
- systems thinking and understanding
- performance understanding
- knowledge of interventions
- business acumen
- organizational understanding
- negotiating/contracting skills
- buy-in/advocacy skills
- coping skills
- ability to see the "big picture"
- consulting skills

Fortunately, most trainers already have adequate-to-excellent skills in many of these areas. Many trainers also have competencies that relate specifically to the analyst role and its outputs (see the chart on the following page).

In the HPI approach, trainers question whether training is the right solution, or even part of the solution, to a performance problem or opportunity. To this day, some trainers exclusively "fill orders" for training requested by others. Meanwhile, most trainers proactively suggest training topics to organizational leaders. But, performance analysis demands looking into nontraining areas and making assessments about their part in achieving performance goals. This is a major shift in thinking for most trainers, the organizational "powers that be," and nontraining staff.

To encourage this shift in your organization, refer to *Info-line* No. 9702, "From Training to Performance Consulting," to help you explain HPI and its advantages to both trainers and upper management.

As ever, sustained top management support is required for a comprehensive shift in strategy and practice. But you can begin simply by adopting the mindset that underlies the HPI process. You can ask questions that encourage others to see the range of intervention possibilities beyond training.

Politely ask *why* someone has requested training, and *what* they want it to achieve. On-the-spot analysis of the answers will help you begin to determine whether training is *how* to go, whether it seems to be a suitable, adequate means for resolving a problem or taking full advantage of an opportunity. If it seems not to be, then you may explain to the person requesting training why you're interested in exploring the extent to which training can accomplish whatever he or she wants to achieve.

## Problem/Opportunity Recognition

*"It isn't that they can't see the solution. It is that they can't see the problem."*

—G.K. Chesterton

Before you can do anything about a problem or opportunity, you must recognize that one exists. Set up a personal plan to scan your organization's environments—internal and external. For example, you might do the following:

**Review performance measures** already available in company documents: annual reports, audits, benchmarking or best practices studies, sales reports, error reports, and so on.

**Build an informal in-house network** of people who speak candidly about performance—and who are more concerned about finding ways to improve it than with finding someone to blame.

**Learn what trend analysts have to say.** Skim business publications to learn what they have to say about workplace change, HPI, and economic trends; attend professional development sessions that cover HPI and forward-looking topics; and watch television shows that feature workplace change and trends.

**Read newspapers, industry publications,** and newsletters to learn of planned changes in staffing, technologies, processes, or legislation related to your organization and its interests.

**Get in the loop for learning** about employee suggestion programs, customer surveys, and supplier requests and complaints.

# Analyst Competencies and Outputs

An HPI analyst conducts trouble-shooting activities to isolate the cause(s) of human performance gaps or conducts activities to identify areas in which human performance can be improved. As shown in the chart below, the analyst's particular competencies may result in a variety of outputs. These outputs enable the analyst to prepare persuasive reports to other people whose support or involvement is needed to correct or prevent performance gaps.

| Competencies | Outputs |
| --- | --- |
| **Performance Analysis Skills (Front-end Analysis):** the process of comparing actual and ideal performance in order to identify gaps and opportunities | • Models and plans to guide troubleshooting of human performance gaps<br>• Work plans to guide performance analysis<br>• Information on trends affecting existing or possible future gaps<br>• Task and job analysis |
| **Needs Analysis Survey Design and Development Skills (Open-ended and Structured):** preparing written, oral, or electronic surveys using open-ended (essay) and closed (scaled) questions to identify HPI needs | • Written (mail) surveys<br>• Oral (phone) surveys<br>• Electronic (e-mail) surveys<br>• Survey administration plans<br>• Research designs<br>• Data analysis and interpretation plans<br>• Reports, statistical summaries, and content analysis summaries of needs analysis surveys |
| **Competency Identification Skills:** identifying the knowledge and skill requirements of teams, jobs, tasks, roles, and work | • Work portfolios and job descriptions<br>• Behavioral events interview guides<br>• Written critical-incident survey questionnaires<br>• Competency models by function, process, origination, or work category<br>• Multi-rater assessments |
| **Questioning Skills:** gathering pertinent information to stimulate insight in individuals and groups through use of interviews and other probing methods | • Interview guides and administration plans<br>• Content analyses of interview results<br>• Team meeting agendas and plans |
| **Analytical Skills (Synthesis):** breaking down the components of a larger whole and reassembling them to achieve improved performance | • Strategies for analyzing the root cause(s) of performance gaps<br>• Fishbone diagrams<br>• Storyboards of problem events |
| **Work Environment Analytical Skills:** examining work environments for issues or characteristics affecting human performance | • Environmental scans<br>• Business/organization plans<br>• Team/group plans<br>• Process improvement strategies/plans |

*Adapted from* ASTD Models for Human Performance, ©1996, ASTD.

**Look for patterns in requests for training.** Does a "solved" problem keep cropping up? If so, chances are, although a symptom of the problem was resolved, its cause has not been uprooted and is sending out new shoots.

**Consider reading *The Futurist*** magazine or joining Internet discussions about the future in general or ongoing developments in the workplace specifically. You may even want to "chat" online with others about workplace change.

## Front-End Analysis

In the January 1996 issue of *Training & Development*, performance-technology pioneer Joe Harless describes a change in emphasis from behavior of employees to an analysis of the desired accomplishments that should result from on-job actions. "It is not just a behavior change that management wants, but an improvement in the output. . . . In the analysis phase, we seek desired accomplishment. This increases the chances that the behaviors we influence are relevant and valuable."

When you become aware of an opportunity or a symptom that represents a problem, review the questions for the analyses described below. Then decide whether you should conduct an informal or formal, full-fledged investigation.

## Assumptions Analysis

Part of analysis is only for you. Answer the following questions to help you determine the assumptions.

☐ What is your own reaction to the problem or opportunity?

☐ What do you believe you know—or can readily find out—about it?

☐ Do you suspect there is more to the problem than you are being told by the person who brought the problem to you?

☐ Can you guess what the unspoken issue is— because you know the sacred cows and taboos of organizational culture?

☐ Are you worried about rocking the boat by bringing up a problem or opportunity?

☐ How hard is it for you to suggest that a solution promoted by others may be not be adequate?

☐ Can you put a positive spin on a search for cause (example: "Yes, that information is a good start. I'll look into that to make sure that we get this thing fixed.")?

☐ Which is a bigger personal risk: delving into cause or offering training that fails to accomplish much—or as much—as it could?

Other questions often are answered in organizational mission and goal statements or have answers implied by past practice. These types of questions are generally as follows:

● How open to change is your organization? How fixed is organizational structure?

● How good are cross-functional relations and communication?

● How are resources allocated to training?

● Is there flexibility in deployment of personnel and job design?

● Do certain problem categories tend to be high priority with management while others are assumed to be unimportant?

● What are the political implications of searching for cause?

● Is management more likely to accept information from someone else to whom you provide background on the problem or opportunity?

Throughout the analysis process, you may find tools such as mind maps, flow charts, or fishbone diagrams useful for capturing and illustrating your growing understanding of a problem or opportunity and its related issues.

# Information Gathering for HPI

To be useful, you will need information that is timely, accurate, relevant, and credible. Specifically, this is information that is corroborated by facts, observations, or agreement among experts, managers, or staff. Once you have gathered and organized this information, you can use it to:

- justify requests for more resources, if needed
- explain why an intervention(s) is recommended
- formulate performance goals and evaluation measures

There are a variety of information resources you can access to gather material. Some of them include the following:

**Company Documents**

- goal/mission statements
- previous performance records
- benchmarking studies
- process diagrams/flow charts
- organizational charts
- budgets and proposed budgets
- strategic planning reports
- quality measures and reports
- production volume and rates
- audits, cost accounting reports
- marketing/advertising plans
- company and customer suggestion program records

**Contracts.** Contracts can be past or current agreements with job performers, suppliers, franchises, consultants, and so forth.

**Subject-Matter Experts.** These are in-house experts, outside consultants, or professors who are acknowledged to have in-depth understanding of areas related to the problem or opportunity.

**Professional Literature.** This includes: books, journals, magazines, and research reports about performance technology or about your organization's industry, especially advancements in tools, techniques, and processes.

**Job Performers.** People whose job performance is to be improved; other job holders whose work affects, or is affected by, those people's performance; those people's managers—and their external customers, if any.

That last item is *not* the least of it: In an August 1996 *Washington Post* report, a 16-year study by Paul Nutt, professor of management science at Ohio State University, assessed the decision-making success of top officials at a number of corporations, government agencies, and non-profit organizations. To be counted as a success, a decision had to be implemented and not reversed in short order. Nutt found that managers who consulted with those who'd be affected by their decisions were more successful; their decisions were carried out 60 percent of the time. Yet this was the least-used style of several that were studied. The most-used style was to issue directives, which attained a 46 percent success rate.

## Information-Gathering Methods

Major methods for gathering HPI information are as follows:

- interviews with individuals (in person or by phone) or focus groups

- written or e-mailed surveys or questionnaires

- observations of individuals or groups

- combined observation and participation, in which one or more job performers talk the analyst through his or her performance of some or all of a job's tasks

## Scope Analysis

Who are the stakeholders—the interested and affected parties—in this problem or opportunity? Does the problem involve or relate to customers, general staff, managers or executives, suppliers, a local community, or the nation? What is the monetary cost—or a ball-park estimate—of the performance gap? If the gap is closed, will time or material be saved and how much of each? Could any potential costs be avoided? Roughly how much is it worth to improve customer relations, staff morale, community goodwill, and organizational reputation related to this problem or opportunity? Are traditional cost-benefit measures applicable in this case? Could the new intangible accounting formulas be helpful?

At this stage, how widespread or limited does the problem or opportunity seem? Can its major effects, side effects, and after effects already be discerned? Is the need for improvement urgent because of a time-sensitive "window of opportunity," safety concerns, loss of income, or deadline imposed by law? What appears to be the growth potential for this problem or opportunity?

## Preliminary Problem/Opportunity Definition

You now have a fairly good handle on what is called the *felt need* or *perceived need*. But, that may be only the tip of the iceberg. Or, the problem may be no larger than it first seems, and yet not be a result of the cause that first comes to mind. There may be multiple causes. At this point, you have a preliminary problem/opportunity definition, but you probably need more information.

Still, as Robert Mager, a leading light in performance technology, has noted, early analyses may reveal that a problem or opportunity is not important enough to pursue. Some problems, although best avoided, are associated with temporary conditions or transitions, and will resolve themselves without intervention and without doing much harm in the meantime.

The ancient Roman motto: *Festina lente* (Make haste slowly) pertains. Work methodically to gather information before drawing a conclusion about whether or how to intervene. In the worst, most time-pressured situations, a methodical approach is more than desirable; it's essential. Keep the military's medical triage officers in mind: They make rapid life-and-death decisions about which soldiers' wounds to treat and in what order. And, they perform amidst bombs and bullets.

## Preliminary Needs Analysis

To determine the constraints and resources available, you will first need to find the answers to the following kinds of questions:

- What resources are there for data gathering?
- How much money is being allocated?
- How many people-hours can be devoted?
- What skills do these people need to have?
- What communications channels are available?
- What machines are available?
- What constrains information gathering?

Often resources and constraints for information gathering are opposite sides of the same coin. For instance, you may have a small budget for proceeding, but it may not be enough. And, company documents, such as union contracts and benchmarking studies, may supply standards and statistics that can be helpful. But these prescriptions and numbers may not be useful because of recently changed circumstances that made earlier standards obsolete, creating a performance gap.

If you believe that you lack adequate resources for full information gathering, you have at least two options. First, if you have the resources with which to begin, you may make an action plan, start gathering information, then use what you find to bolster your case in a request for resources to continue.

Second, if you believe that resources are insufficient for a respectable headstart, or that starting without adequate resources will make you look like a poor planner, you will need to develop a persuasive request for resources right away. Decide to whom this request should be directed. Then decide how to approach that person or those people—in a special written report, in a regular quarterly report, in an upcoming budget-setting process, in one-on-one or group meetings, and so on.

## Needs and Cause Analysis

The needs to be considered fall into several categories. In their book, *Performance Consulting: Moving Beyond Training*, Dana Gaines Robinson and James C. Robinson describe the following:

- business needs that relate to goals for a unit, department, or organization

- performance needs that relate to on-the-job behavioral requirements of a person or people performing a particular job; in other words, what people need to do to meet business needs

- work environment needs that relate to systems, processes, conditions, and tools required to support successful performance

- training needs that relate to what people must learn if they are to perform successfully

- customer needs and wants that are the impetus for business needs

Joe Harless has said that interventions to improve performance may provide information, for example, through instruction or job aids. Interventions can also cause the following to occur:

- a change in the work environment, perhaps through work redesign, provision of better tools, or changes in lighting

- a change in motivational or incentive conditions (through feedback, recognition, or various forms of compensation)

- a change selection or assignment of human resources (by new hiring or assignment practices, or reassignment of people to jobs that draw on their strongest competencies)

Watch for and ask about performance gaps related to those categories. You may quickly discover what seems to be a completely obvious cause for a gap. If an uncomplicated or inexpensive intervention seems to be an equally obvious response, recommend trying the lower cost approach before going into further analyses. But in your recommendation, avoid saying that the intervention will take care of the matter once and for all. If evaluations show that the intervention helps—but not enough—you will want to have left the door open for extending your investigation.

## Meeting Performance Related Changes

To meet needs, changes may be required at one or more levels: organization, process, individual, or team. For example, an organization may offer counter-productive "incentives," a process may have evolved through a series of quick-fix add-ons that make it unduly complex, or job performers may need practice in a once-infrequent task that will be used more often in the future. As previously mentioned, HPI uses approaches, tools, and techniques from many fields.

For advice on change at the various levels, look into the existing literature about organizational development, especially diagnosis and organizational transitions and transformation; reengineering; process improvement and innovation; teamwork; and work-related motivations and incentives.

Make it clear that information indicating how to improve performance is your interest. Take care to avoid putting anyone on the defensive. Speak of *problems*, not *failures*. Naturally, people whose performance or decisions about performance are under scrutiny may be fearful, angry, or otherwise distressed by the implication that they may be blameworthy. But, they usually will warm up to and welcome an opportunity to tell their ideas for improving the areas in which they work. And, your attention to tools and work settings will show that you are looking at the "big picture."

In analyzing performance improvement needs and their causes, examine the answers to these categories of questions:

### ■ *Individual Performance Analysis*

How many people's performance will be analyzed? Do they have the same or different job titles? Are they in one functional area or across functions? Is a job cluster involved?

### ■ *Job Performance and Location*

If the job performers are in different functional areas, do they share job-related language and values? Where are the job performers—physically, geographically? How good is your access to them—physically and in terms of their having time to respond to interviews, surveys, and so on. When do they work—more or less 9-to-5, or in shifts into or over the night?

### ■ *Interdepartmental Performance*

Is there a history of cooperation or competition between or among the functional areas? If the latter, has the competition been productive or counterproductive? Have new circumstances—such as a reorganization—altered functional relationships?

### ■ *Physical Setting Performance*

What is or are the setting(s) for job performance—offices, factories, warehouses, retail outlets? What are the conditions there—noisy or quiet; stuffy or well-ventilated; hot, cold, or moderate; damp, humid, or neutral in air quality; with dim, bright, or moderate lighting; and so forth? Slightly dim lights may make it easier for people who read computer screens, but dim lights in an inspection area would likely be the cause or a contributing cause of a problem there.

### ■ *Tools and Equipment Performance*

What tools, supplies, or raw materials are needed to perform the job? Are those things in good condition and up to date? Would it help explain problems to upper management if you took photographs of working conditions, tools, and equipment? If tools and equipment are in good shape, are they "mainstream" in capabilities? Are they obsolete compared to what competitors use? Do the people who use them know how to operate them to full advantage? What is the procedure for getting training? Is it efficient from the user's point of view?

### ■ *Physical Performance*

How do job performers vary in individual physical capacity for doing the job under current conditions with current tools and equipment? Do some people need "left-handed" tools? Do some people prefer a track-ball to a mouse for use with computer software? Would people be more comfortable if desks, tables, or equipment platforms were lowered or raised? Keep in mind that at any given time nearly one-third of American adults either need glasses or contact lenses or a new prescription for the ones they have.

### ■ *Employee Appraisal Performance*

How long have these people performed their jobs? How long have they been in your organization? Are there many newcomers or people about to retire? How have their appraisals been? What measures are appraisal based on? Are there patterns or trends in appraisal of what people do and how they do it? Even if appraisal documentation is available to you, you may want to ask managers and job performers for their perspectives on recent appraisals.

### ■ *Hiring and Process Performance*

If your organization has had a hiring freeze or undergone downsizing, what has that done to job design, morale, and work flow? Are there emergency or contingency plans for this job or process? Have they been used? If so, when and with what results?

### ■ *Benchmarking Performance*

Can or should you talk with, survey, or observe all the job performers? What about their managers? If not, how will you select a sample? Which performers have been identified by managers or colleagues as exemplary? If, because of a performance gap, no one is considered exemplary, does anyone still have a reputation for better results than most? Who's considered to be a typical performer? Are you able to analyze and assess all parts of the job(s) to be performed, or do you need expert advice or help? Focus on how to improve the performance of typical workers.

■ *Compensation Performance*

What happens to people who are very productive? Are they rewarded? Are they, in effect, punished by being given more work for no reward? Are good, average, and poor performers given feedback to let them know how their performance stacks up? Are they offered help for improvement? Do managers and supervisors model, support, or reinforce application of skills and adherence to approved procedures?

Are managers and supervisors able and willing to coach performers who report to them? Do people have to ask for help? Is there time to give it to them on the job? Are there mixed messages in standards? For instance, are job performers responsible for quality that can't humanly be achieved within the time allotted? Or, are there values conflicts? For instance, does management want quick-and-dirty mock-ups of new products being considered for production, rough drafts of advertisements, and so on (because these may never go farther), while the people who create these "believe in" a slower, well-crafted approach?

■ *Models for Performance*

Is there a performance model for the job(s)? Was it designed in-house or did it come from a professional society or "best practices" study by the government, a consulting group, or a university? Have competencies for this job been listed or described? These matters are of particular concern when new jobs are being created.

■ *Skills Performance*

How consistent are the job's knowledge and skill demands? Are there tasks that are performed infrequently? Are there work rushes and slow periods? Is everything nearly always done in a rush? Is this the nature of the job, or is it a symptom of a problem in planning, scheduling, or receipt of work orders or materials?

Have the knowledge, skills, and attitudes required for performance been translated into behavioral objectives that can be measured or observed? If not, begin the formulation of objectives, which won't be completed until the intervention phase of HPI. Additionally, does job analysis and the study of the relationships among jobs seem to provide enough detail? Should task analysis be done as well?

---

## So, What's the Problem?

In the list below, can you identify which items represent problems and which ones represent opportunities?

- rising expenses
- loss of customers or customer complaints
- loss of suppliers or supplier complaints
- operational inefficiencies
- heightened competition
- staffing concerns such as turnover or absenteeism
- accidents that injure people, destroy data or machinery
- decreasing sales or production
- increasing back orders or out-of-stock situations
- too many or too few supplies or raw materials
- too much or inaccurate inventory
- delayed, untimely decision making
- changes in—or introduction of new—products or services
- introduction of new technologies, processes, forms

The last two items in the list represent opportunities. All the others are *symptoms* that represent problems. And, by nature, problems offer opportunity for improvement. Sometimes, a problem will, upon analysis, prove more serious, widespread, or deep-rooted than the symptom that first caught attention. Other problems, although as serious as their symptoms indicate, are readily resolved—if their cause(s) are known.

---

If training seems to be all or part of the response to a performance gap, will the training be required or voluntary? Where will it be conducted? For how long? During the regular work period or on overtime? What bearing do trainees' cultural heritages have on selection of means for instruction? For example, are they from a background in which questioning a teacher or trainer would be considered rude? What earlier education or training and development have they had? How well do they read? What general and job-specific vocabulary do they have?

Will the training that job performers have received result in, or be followed up by, outside testing for certification or licensing. What standards are required by the certification or licensing agency?

## Information Gathering

As you gather information, be thinking about likely explanations for what's been going badly or well. Look for *causal links* or *bridges*. In a particular situation, there may be no direct cause-and-effect, just a combination of factors that enhance or detract from desired performance.

You will also want to look for what is different about the situation. Do not assume that a new problem is just like an earlier one. It is possible that the current situation has a small but crucial difference. Scratch beneath the surface to look for any distinctions.

In answering needs analysis questions, you will learn:

- who is involved
- where they work
- under what conditions they work

In addition to questioning what is happening, you also should question what is *not* happening, but should be. Perhaps a process is overefficient; a little double-checking or duplication here and there might save time and errors in the long run. Also, what "missing" tools and equipment are not crucial, but could lead to cost-effective improvement? At this point, you only need to consider what might help and how; questions about feasibility and cost-benefit are taken up later. But, record the questions that come to mind.

Look for timing that is associated with variations in performance:

- Does the problem arise only occasionally?

- Is the problem seasonal?

- Is the problem more likely to occur mornings, afternoons, or on weekends?

Also look outside the organization for causes of performance gaps:

- Are suppliers late with deliveries?

- Do distributors follow good marketing practices?

- Are customers failing to follow the directions that accompany the product?

Each of these situations still has a tie to an "inside position" that exists or probably should—there is always a person who is accountable for supplier selection and contract compliance. Additionally, someone is responsible for marketing to distributors; and somebody writes product directions and decides how big they should be and where to put them.

External causes—short of terrorist attacks, natural disasters, and regional or national calamities (such as loss of a region's principal employer whose workers were the bulk of your customers, or a stock market crash)—are generally correctable from inside the organization. Even in bad times, improvement is possible, perhaps by finding new customers to market to or by making an innovative leap. Henry Luce did fine when he began *Time* magazine just as the Depression came along. Faint heart never won market share.

One technique for seeking cause is *backward chaining*. Mentally work backwards from the end of a process or from an end product or service. What was the step before the last step? The one before that? Keep at it until (maybe) you hit a snag or find a gap.

## Goals Analysis

For performance related to a problem or opportunity, what behaviors are required, desirable, or optional? If current performance results are mixed, what aspects of performance should be preserved ("not throwing out the baby with the bath water")? In an ideal improvement, what will be increased—productivity, innovation, goodwill, return on shares? What will be reduced—rework, delays, accidents, complaints? Are there critical performance requirements that, if lacking, spell failure? Are there basic performance standards that, although lower than optimal achievement, would move performance from inadequate to adequate? What must or could an intervention accomplish or achieve? In other words, what would a successful outcome look like?

## Risk Analysis

Risks and potential risks that can be anticipated typically should be handled through preventive measures, protective ones, or both. As you assess risk, question whether the costs of prevention and protection measures are in keeping with the goals and scope of the problem or opportunity.

Also think about what is likely to happen if nothing is done to offset a given risk. Assess what the costs (time, money, morale, good will, productivity—even lost lives) might be if:

- equipment failed or malfunctioned
- new equipment did not arrive when expected
- a job performer skipped a step in a process
- the lights, heat, or air conditioning went out

Except when a situation clearly has potential for serious health and safety risks, do not develop a worst-case scenario; but look for and ask about what is going right that sometimes goes wrong, or easily could go wrong.

What potential pitfalls and risks can an intervention prevent? How? For example, if you're aware of stakeholders' concerns, a candid, credible communication plan to address these may forestall most resistance to change. You will also need to look at what risks cannot be avoided. What protective actions could still reduce risk—phased introduction of changes to allow for monitoring and swift reaction to negative, unintended effects; insurance for new equipment; legal advice on wording of contracts?

Later, when developing interventions, it's wiser to employ more than one method for dealing with actual and potential risks. For example, an information-intensive office might improve data security by providing training about computer or data security measures, using surge suppressors, implementing procedures to deter unauthorized access to data, using software with built-in "save" functions, and storing duplicates of essential data at an off-site location.

## Needs Analysis Know-How

In *Strategic Thinking: A Guide to Identifying and Solving Problems,* author Roger Kaufman offers the following guidelines for thinking, talking, and writing about performance needs:

- Define a need as a gap between current and desired results—not as insufficient resources, means, or "how-to-do-its."

- Distinguish between needs and wants.

- Prioritize needs in order to focus on the most important.

- Steer clear of the phrases *need to, in need of, need for, needed,* and *needing.* They lead to conclusion-jumping caused by equating a problem with its solution. Instead, use "need" as a noun. For instance, say: "The primary need is to find ways to improve cross-functional communications" as opposed to "We need to reorganize."

Kaufman also classifies four scales of measurement:

1. Nominal: name or label; in measuring and evaluating some performance behaviors, it's only possible to name an action and then note whether it did or didn't happen.

2. Ordinal: ranking as *greater, equal, less desirable,* and so on—without saying, for instance, how much greater.

3. Interval: ranking by markers of equal variation from an arbitrary point, such as plus or minus dollars of sales from a sales-projection target.

4. Ratio: similar to interval except that the point of comparison occurs naturally, such as the zero freezing-point of water in the centigrade temperature scale.

These scales may measure performance gaps (describe performance needs) or achievement (evaluate whether or how well needs have been met). Kaufman cautions against using a scale that's inappropriate to what's being measured. He says that interval-scale terms are the most precise scale generally applicable to human behavior.

## Definition Refined; Resources Revisited

By now boundaries have been put on the preliminary problem or opportunity definition. This narrows the range of possible interventions to ones likely to succeed in filling gaps and attaining goals. In many cases, an analyst prepares a report or two at this stage. One report may:

- Define the problem or opportunity as it is presently understood.

- Describe the problem's scope and impact.

- Present major findings thus far—about needs, work conditions, tools, causal links, and so on.

- Request permission and resources to move to the remaining phases of HPI.

Or, this report may conclude that the performance problem essentially was solved in the course of analysis for cause. Remember that the original "bug" in a computer system was an insect; once removed, the problem was solved. This type of report or request goes to decision makers who will add their perspectives to the process.

A second report would go into much more detail, organizing and presenting virtually all the findings to date. Decision makers should be told that this report is being put together, but they usually do not want this much detail. Whoever generates the intervention will want and need this information. If you are to carry out those phases, you may not need to write narrative explanations for data—but, they would be a back-up in case someone else needed to take over. Make sure that you have captured pertinent information in writing, graphs, or pictures and that information is organized for easy retrieval. At the least, number items—documents, survey summaries, observation results, and so on—and then prepare a list the items. Make one or two copies of this report, and maintain one copy off site.

# Intervention, Change, Evaluation

*"Success in solving the problem depends on choosing the right aspect, on attacking the fortress from its accessible side."*

—George Polya

After the analysis phase of HPI comes the generation of alternative interventions and the selection of interventions(s) and related implementation and evaluation strategies. In the intervention phase, measurable or observable behavioral objectives are devised by interpretation and combination of the facts, observations, and opinions gathered in the analysis phase. These objectives are tied to business and performance goals and are the basis of evaluation.

Part of the intervention phase is consideration of demands and effects on the overall organization. For example, will a possible intervention change lines of authority and accountability? Is a particular intervention feasible? Are enough time, money, and so forth available to implement it? Is it *possible*? Belling the cat would have saved the mice grief, if a mouse martyr or two *could* have done it. Besides (apologies for the cruel metaphor), there's more than one way to skin a cat. Consideration also is given to how job performers are likely to react to proposed changes. Sometimes, a trial run or limited pilot test helps test the suitability of a recommended intervention.

The implementation and change management phases of HPI go hand-in-hand. And, the evaluation phase of HPI assesses both the improvement that an intervention brings while underway, and has brought after a "new" process, tool, skill application, or whatever has become routine. Straight successes rarely result, but continuous improvement is frequent, and major improvement is not infrequent. As time moves on, new challenges arise, so the environmental scanning of the analysis phase continues.

## Performance in Evolution

Performance technology and human performance improvement are evolving. They have been, and are, influenced by lessons learned in the development of computer systems and in the search for ways to make those systems pay off.

HPI relates to a movement toward *resources integration*, in which the management and development of human, information, material, and capital resources are considered in the context of one another. In resources integration, particular attention is paid to interfaces—where resources overlap or connect effectively and efficiently, or fail to. As a result, problems develop or opportunities fall between the cracks.

Geary A. Rummler and Alan P. Brache have written extensively about the cracks, the *white space* in organizations. They have said that all organization structures have white space, so the mission is not to eliminate white space. The mission is "to minimize the extent to which white space impedes processes and to manage the white space that must exist."

When computer scientists set out to create computers that could learn (as indicated by ability to perform better), the scientists discovered that they needed to know more about how humans think and learn. Thus, the field of cognitive science was born. This expanding field has researched learning from the level of changes in brain chemistry to the psychology of motivation.

Although the expression *Information Age* remains current, it is joined by references to the global, *knowledge-based economy*. In this economy, organizational success often rests on management and development of *intellectual assets* (also known as *intellectual capital*). These assets are embodied in people and embedded in processes and documents. Learning and creativity—for improvement or innovation—enhance and increase intellectual assets.

Former ASTD president Gloria Regalbuto has pointed out that trainers who conduct analyses for HPI codify knowledge and tasks. They determine, describe, and document such things as optimal performance techniques and sequences or essential and desirable performance competencies. This makes their work valuable in the knowledge-based economy.

# References & Resources

## Articles

Barron, Tom. "The Road Toward Performance: Three Vignettes." *Technical & Skills Training,* January 1997, pp. 12-14.

Carnevale, A.P., and E.R. Shulz. "Return on Investment: Accounting for Training." *Training & Development,* July 1990, pp. 41/S-1-S-30.

Carnevale, Ellen S. "The Questions and the Answers: An Interview with Robert Mager." *Technical & Skills Training,* July 1992, pp. 14-17.

Carr, C., and L. Totzke. "The Long and Winding Path (From Instructional Technology to Performance Technology)." *Performance & Instruction,* August 1995, pp. 4-8.

Byrne, J.A. "Strategic Planning." *Business Week,* August 26, 1996, pp. 46-52.

Davis, S., and J. Botkin. "The Coming of Knowledge-Based Business." *Harvard Business Review,* Vol. 72, No. 75, Sept. 1994, pp. 165-170.

Dean, Peter J., et al. "Employee Perceptions of Workplace Factors that Will Most Improve Their Performance." *Performance Improvement Quarterly,* Vol. 9, No. 2 (1996), pp. 75-89.

Denton, David W. "Don't Hire Performance Problems: The Employment Interview and the Performance Improvement Practitioner." *Performance Improvement,* October 1996, pp. 6-9.

Hallberg, Cliff, and Rich DeFiore. "Curving Toward Performance." *Technical & Skills Training,* January 1997, pp. 9-11.

Harless, Joe. "Whither Performance Technology?" *Performance & Instruction,* Vol. 31, No. 2, February 1992, pp. 4-8.

Harless, J. "Performance Technology Skills in Business: Implications for Preparation." *Performance Improvement Quarterly,* Vol. 8, No. 5 (1995), pp. 75-88.

Kaplan, Robert S., and David P. Norton. "Strategic Learning and the Balanced Scorecard." *Strategy & Leadership,* September/October 1996, pp. 18-24.

Middlebrook, John F. "How to Manage Individual Performance." *Training & Development,* September 1996, pp. 45-48.

"Performance Consulting: Proving an Idea with Appeal Also Has a Pay-off." *Training Directors' Forum Newsletter,* October 1996, pp. 1-3.

Reuters (news service). "Consulting from Above." *The Washington Post,* August 18, 1996, p. H4.

Ricciardi, Philip. "Simplify Your Approach to Performance Management: Use This Model to Provide Equitable Measures of Productivity and Quality for Employees in All Departments." *HRMagazine,* March 1996, pp. 98-106.

Rosenof, Rhonda. "Multiple Delivery Strategies and Changing Business Demands." *CBT Solutions,* May/June 1996, pp. 28-32.

Rummler, Geary A. "In Search of the Holy Performance Grail." *Training & Development,* April 1996, pp. 26-32.

Sleezer, C.M. "Tried and True Performance Analysis." *Training and Development,* Vol. 47, No. 11, November 1993, pp. 52-54.

Sorohan, Erica Gordon. "The Performance Consultant at Work." *Training & Development,* March 1996, pp. 34-38.

Spitzer, Dean R. "Ensuring Successful Performance Improvement Interventions." *Performance Improvement,* October 1996, pp. 26-27.

Swoboda, F. "Turning Paychecks Into a Performance Art." *The Washington Post,* August 25, 1996, p. H4.

Thor, Carl G. "Using a Family of Measures to Assess Organizational Performance." *National Productivity Review,* Summer 1995, pp. 111-131.

## Audiotapes

Broad, Mary, and Steve Seitz. *Transfer of Learning: Stakeholder Partnerships to Support Full Performance.* ASTD audiotape 96AST-S7.

McRae, Elaine. *Training Needs Analysis: A Quick Performance-Based, Consultative Approach.* ASTD audiotape 96AST-S25.

Regalbuto, Gloria. *The Front End of Front-End Analysis.* ASTD audiotape 95AST-M68.

Robinson, James, William Rothwell, and Marc Rosenberg. *Strategies for Improving Human Performance.* ASTD audiotape 96AST-W17.

Rothwell, William, and David Dubois. *Helping Your Organization Become a High Performance Workplace.* ASTD audiotape 96AST-M3.

Rummler, Geary. *Linking Training and Performance.* ASTD audiotape 96AST-S12.

Taylor, Doug, and Eileen Dello-Martin. *Creating a Continuous Improvement Strategy for Your Organization.* ASTD audiotape 96AST-W39.

## Books

ASTD. *Introduction to Performance: A Primer for Trainers.* Alexandria, Virginia: American Society for Training & Development, 1996.

———. *The Best of Performance Support in the Workplace.* Alexandria, Virginia: American Society for Training & Development, 1994.

Brown, Mark Graham, et al. *Rx For Business: A Troubleshooting Guide for Building a High Performance Organization.* Chicago, Illinois: Irwin Professional Publishing, 1996.

Dean, Peter J., (ed). *Performance Engineering at Work.* Batavia, Illinois: International Board of Standards for Training, Performance and Instruction, 1994.

Harless, Joe H. *Analyzing Human Performance: Tools for Achieving Business Results.* Alexandria, Virginia, and Annapolis, Maryland: American Society for Training & Development and Human Performance Technologies, 1997.

Higgins, J.M. *101 Creative Problem Solving Techniques: The Handbook of New Ideas for Business.* Winter Park, Florida: The New Management Publishing Company, 1994.

Howard, Pierce J. *The Owner's Manual for the Brain: Everyday Applications from Mind-Brain Research.* Austin, Texas: Leornian Press, 1994.

Kaufman, Roger. *"Assessing Needs," Introduction to Identifying and Solving Problems.* Alexandria, Virginia: American Society for Training & Development and the International Society for Performance Improvement, 1996.

———. *Strategic Thinking: A Guide to Identifying and Solving Problems.* Alexandria, Virginia: American Society for Training & Development and International Society for Performance Improvement, 1996.

Landon, Danny G. *The New Language of Work.* Amherst, Massachusetts: HRD Press, 1995.

Mager, Robert F. *Making Instruction Work.* Belmont, California: David S. Lake Publishers, 1988.

———. *What Every Manager Should Know about Training or "I've Got a Training Problem" and Other Odd Ideas.* Belmont, California: Lake Publishing, 1992.

Porter, Michael E. *Competitive Advantage: Creating and Sustaining Superior Performance.* New York: The Free Press, 1985.

Robinson, Dana G., and James C. Robinson. *Performance Consulting: Moving Beyond Training.* San Francisco: Berrett-Koehler, 1995.

Rossett, A. *Training Needs Assessment.* Englewood Cliffs, New Jersey: Educational Technology Publications, 1990.

Rothwell, William J. *ASTD Models for Human Performance.* Alexandria, Virginia: American Society for Training & Development, 1996.

Rummler, Geary A., and Alan P. Brache. *Improving Performance: Managing the White Space on the Organization Chart.* San Francisco: Jossey-Bass, 1996.

Stolovitch, H.D., and E.J. Keeps. *Handbook of Human Performance Technology: A Comprehensive Guide for Analyzing and Solving Performance Problems in Organizations.* San Francisco: Jossey-Bass, 1992.

Swanson, Richard A. *Analysis for Improving Performance: Tools for Diagnosing Organizations and Documenting Workplace Expertise.* San Francisco: Berrett-Koehler, 1996.

## Info-lines

Austin, M. "Needs Assessment by Focus Group." No. 9401 (revised 1998).

Bricker, B. "Training Basics: Basics of Performance Technology." No. 9211 (out of print).

Butruille, S.G. "Be a Better Job Analyst." No. 8903 (revised 1998).

Callahan, Madelyn. "Be a Better Needs Analyst." No. 8502 (revised 1998).

———. "Write Better Behavioral Objectives." No. 8505 (revised 1998).

———. "Performance Consulting." No. 9702.

Chang, R.Y. "Continuous Process Improvement." No. 9210.

Gill, S.J. "Linking Training to Performance Goals." No. 9606 (revised 1998).

Hodell, Chuck. "Basics of Instructional Systems Development." No. 9706.

Waagen, Alice. "Essentials for Evaluation." No. 9705.

## Job Aid

# A Human Performance Improvement Analysis Checklist

Use this checklist to review the steps to take in analysis for human performance improvement.

☐ Monitor and analyze internal and external organizational environments.

☐ Look for problems (or their symptoms) and opportunities for human performance improvement.

☐ Conduct preliminary analyses of:

☐ assumptions
☐ the problem/opportunity's scope (how serious, widespread, and likely to grow)
☐ resources/constraints for information gathering

☐ Develop a preliminary problem definition.

☐ Gather additional information from:

☐ documents
☐ experts, if necessary

☐ Decide whether to use:

☐ face-to-face or telephone interviews
☐ written or e-mailed surveys/questionnaires
☐ observations

☐ Select job performers and others from whom to gather information.

☐ Look for problems related to job performers':

☐ information or knowledge
☐ work environment (setting, tools, processes)
☐ motivation or incentives
☐ selection and assignment

☐ Consider whether the root of the problem is at the organizational level.

☐ Consider the influence that people outside the organization have on the problem—and, the influence that the problem has on them.

☐ Analyze problem/opportunity for cause, side effects, and consequences.

☐ Define goals for performance improvement.

☐ Anticipate risks; consider preventive and protective measures.

☐ Consider whether more information gathered about the scope of the gaps in performance (and related goals and risks) requires redefinition of the problem.

☐ Prepare summary report of findings and request for resources for working on intervention generation and selection.

☐ Record and organize current findings for easy retrieval of information.

☐ Devise and follow an action plan for learning more about HPI and performance technology.

☐ Continue to monitor internal and external organizational environments.

# The Role of the Performance Intervention Specialist

Issue 9714

# The Role of the Performance Intervention Specialist

AUTHOR:

Madelyn R. Callahan

## Performance

**Editorial Staff for 9714**

**Editor**
Cat Sharpe

**Associate Editor**
Patrick McHugh

**Designer**
Steven M. Blackwood

**Copy Editor**
Kay Larson

# The Intervention Specialist

*To design performance improvement interventions powerful enough to produce long-term change, it helps to keep in mind two concepts grounded in the physical sciences. The first is inertia, the tendency to resist change; the second is entropy, the tendency toward chaos…*

—Dean R. Spitzer

Human performance improvement (HPI) involves identifying performance gaps, examining interventions that could close those gaps, selecting the best interventions for the job, and evaluating their effectiveness in closing the performance gaps. In the sequence of steps for the HPI process, intervention falls after the performance analysis phase but before implementation and evaluation. Not surprisingly, the transition from one step to the next may include some degree of overlap between phases, which may similarly affect the corresponding HPI roles of analyst, intervention specialist, change manager, and evaluator.

In this issue of *Info-line* you will have a detailed look at the role of the intervention specialist in the human performance improvement process. This close examination will describe what the intervention specialist does, the skills required to do the job, and how the specialist's role complements the other HPI roles.

How the process works for a specific application may affect the relationships between the various roles. The four phases of the process may occur in sequence, or two or more of the phases may take place simultaneously, which is where phases and roles may overlap. This is especially true of the role of the intervention specialist. While the specialist's primary function is to choose the best interventions to address problems or situations causing gaps between real and ideal performance, there are also aspects of the job that involve performance and cause analysis, implementation, and change management.

This *Info-line* will also discuss the types of interventions and various levels of intervention. It will provide guidelines on planning an intervention project by asking the right questions about the scope, resources, and limitations of the project. It will also explain how to put together and facilitate an intervention, what competencies are required of an intervention specialist, and what the experts suggest to boost the potential for success.

# The Role

The primary job of the intervention specialist is to research root causes of past, current, and possible performance gaps with the goal of closing those gaps. But the specialist will likely become involved with other phases of the process as well: the front-end needs analysis, solution design, development, implementation, and evaluation.

In some cases the specialist may find that the client has already completed some or most of these phases. At other times the specialist may be responsible for the entire process. Single interventions or combinations of them may be used, depending on the kinds and amounts of root causes that must be addressed.

Following are the key activities an intervention specialist may participate in:

■ *Problem Identification*
If the performance problem is unknown, the specialist may assist the analyst in conducting a needs analysis.

■ *Problem Analysis*
Once the performance problem is specified, the specialist may assist the analyst in trying to determine the causes of the problem by looking at each part and classifying factors related to it.

■ *Intervention Design*
If the problem has been identified based on thorough analysis, the specialist may then review the data to begin planning the design. The process requires identifying specific elements for each solution. Working with these specifications involves drawing on expertise in the areas of management consulting, organizational development, training and instructional design, and personnel management.

■ *Intervention Development*
Given the specifications for the solution, the specialist may begin the process of actually putting together the intervention. The project may include gathering materials, drafting schedules, preparing activities, and so forth.

■ *Aiding Intervention Implementation*
Once the solution has been designed, the specialist may be called on to help the change manager put it in place. Examples of solutions include providing training based on comprehensive guidelines, producing and disseminating job aids and other tools, or taking a leadership position in a program to improve quality or productivity.

## Competency Requirements

Here are some of the competencies that are key to being a successful intervention specialist.

**Interpreting performance information.** This involves being able to draw practical meaning from the analysis data and it also involves assisting other professionals who do so including performers, those who manage performers, and all others who have invested in the intervention process .

**Selecting interventions.** This requires picking the appropriate human performance improvement intervention to get at the underlying root causes, instead of the symptoms, of the performance gap.

**Interpreting changes in performance.** This entails predicting and examining the impact and results of interventions.

**Assessing relationships between interventions.** This requires analyzing the impact of various interventions on the organization's departments and the organization's relationship with clients, employees, suppliers, and distributors.

**Identifying key business concerns.** This involves the ability to locate information that is critical to business operations and applying it during the performance improvement intervention.

# Outputs and Competencies Associated with the Intervention Specialist

| Competencies | Enabling Outputs | Terminal Outputs |
|---|---|---|
| **Performance Information Interpretation Skills:** finding useful meaning from the results of performance analysis; helping performers, performers' managers, process owners, and other stakeholders to do so | **Intervention Selection Skills:** selecting HPI interventions that address the root cause(s) of performance gaps rather than symptoms or side effects | **Change Interpretation Skills:** forecasting and analyzing the effects of interventions and their consequences |
| • Written or oral briefings to performers, performers' managers, process owners, or other stakeholders about the results of performance or cause analysis | • Approaches for choosing appropriate HPI strategies to close performance gaps | • Written and oral briefings to performers, performers' managers, process owners, and other stakeholders about the likely impact of change or of an HPI intervention on processes, individuals, or the organization |
| • Useful information drawn from performance or cause analysis | | • Problem-solving activities to lead performers, performers' managers, process owners, and other stakeholders to discover or forecast the impact of an intervention's implementation on processes, individuals, or the organization |
| • Persuasive reports to stakeholders about the appropriate intervention(s) to close past, present, or future performance gap(s) | | |

**Implementing goals.** This encompasses translating goals into effective action that will close current or potential performance gaps; it also involves being able to achieve goals despite obstacles such as scarce resources and conflicts regarding priorities.

## Improving Competency Levels

Intervention specialists and other HPI professionals can develop their HPI competencies and skills by taking advantage of local and professional resources such as:

- sharing information with others in the field

- selecting a role model and emulating that person

- engaging in short- or long-term projects with others in the field

- taking courses or nondegree continuing education seminars at nearby colleges or universities

- tapping into electronic or people networks

- keeping up with professional reading of books, newsletters, journals, and periodicals

- using self-teaching tools such as videotapes, audiotapes, software, and other multimedia-based learning materials

- working with professional associations

---

## Competencies

**Ability to Assess Relationships Among Interventions:** examining the effects of multiple HPI interventions on parts of an organization, as well as the effects on the organization's interactions with customers, suppliers, distributors, and workers

- Written and oral briefings to performers, performers' managers, process owners, and other stakeholders about the likely impact of multiple interventions on processes, individuals, or the organization

- Problem-solving activities to lead performers, performers' managers, process owners, and other stakeholders to discover or forecast the likely impact of multiple interventions on processes, individuals or the organization

## Enabling Outputs

**Ability to Identify Critical Business Issues and Changes:** determining key business issues and applying that information during the implementation of a human performance improvement intervention

- Organizational analyses

- Process analyses

- White papers on human performance improvement strategies

- Oral and written briefings to performers, performers' managers, process owners, and stakeholders about possible improvement strategies

- Customer satisfaction information and survey results

## Terminal Outputs

**Goal Implementation Skills:** ensuring that goals are converted effectively into actions to close existing or pending performance gaps; getting results despite conflicting priorities, lack of resources, or ambiguity

- Written or oral goals for HPI

- Performance objectives for the interventions

- Facilitate performance objectives

*Adapted from* ASTD Models for Human Performance *by William Rothwell, 1996.*

## Proposing an Intervention

An intervention specialist may be called on to draft or contribute to a proposal for intervention, which is a contract that spells out the specialist's plan of action. This plan is presented to the client as an agreement to proceed with the performance improvement project. It may be part of a plan or the initial piece of a more detailed plan to be submitted later.

The proposal provides a general outline and includes the following elements:

■ *Performance Gap Statement*
The performance requirement should be stated in terms that describe and compare the current performance level with organizational goals and expectations for performance and with the ideal or anticipated performance levels after the performance improvement intervention.

■ *Performance Analysis Statement*
Along with describing the gap between real and ideal performance, include a succinct interpretation of why the performance gap exists. Some reasons may include: lack of knowledge or skill, poor aptitude, absence of incentives, or problem work environment. Performance variables that should be identified in the diagnosis include: mission or goal, systems design, capacity, motivation, and expertise.

■ *Recommendation Statement*
In response to multifaceted performance problems, interventions should be multidimensional. State recommended interventions in terms specifying that they are based on: suitability to the organization's culture and heritage, project availability, design quality, proven effectiveness, cost, and anticipated benefits.

■ *Expected Benefits Statement*
This should explain both the monetary and non-monetary performance value or gains in terms of the outcome of closing the gap between the current and required performance levels. Financial statements of benefits are based on an established performance value less costs of the performance improvement efforts. Pre- and postintervention benefits, costs, and values of performance should be compared to provide a full picture of the anticipated performance gains.

## Internal and External Consultants

In some situations, the best way to facilitate the intervention process is by having two intervention specialists—one on staff inside the organization and one outside consultant. Alone, the internal specialist may have difficulty trying to effectively promote interventions within the organization. Often the internal specialist's recommendations are overlooked until they've been voiced by an external consultant.

The job of the external specialist is to advocate the solution and see it through to acceptance by decision makers. Inside the organization, the internal specialist, who has the advantage of knowing who to contact and how to get things done, acts as

---

# Planning: A Key Competency

According to William J. Rothwell in *ASTD Models for Human Performance Improvement,* a valuable core competency for intervention specialists is having a broad-based knowledge of interventions. This requires understanding the various ways to improve performance in an organization and demonstrating how to apply the different kinds of interventions to close current and future performance gaps.

The intervention specialist must be able to plan:

- recruitment or selection programs
- orientation programs
- training programs
- performance appraisal programs
- career development programs
- organization development interventions
- compensation, reward, and incentive programs
- employee feedback programs
- employee discipline programs
- employee counseling and wellness programs
- safety programs
- improved tools and equipment
- improved on-the-job training
- improved on-the-job learning
- job aids
- organizational design
- task design
- ergonomic improvements
- improved employee staff and forecasting programs
- other HPI strategies and interventions

change agent and shepherds the project through the various channels and resource personnel. The problem for external consultants functioning as change agents is that they're perceived as owning the intervention, so once they leave, the impetus for making and continuing changes goes with them. As peoples' enthusiasm for the project wanes, so may their support and interest. Chances are the project and its effects will gradually come to an end.

A good partnership between the specialists ensures against failure of the project. This is especially important from the staff specialist's point of view since the job of working inside can be more challenging. Internal consultants are likely to have more hands-on dealings with people's reluctance to change and their resulting anger, frustration, and resentment. Often the internal specialist may be concerned that the organization takes for granted the skills and strengths required to deal with a difficult workforce during interventions.

Internal consultants may also see inequity in the fact that the external consultant's job seems much less stressful. After the external consultant makes a recommendation for an intervention and it's been accepted, it becomes the responsibility of the staff specialist to carry out the intervention and put it in place. Because of situations like this, it is crucial for for the two specialists to cooperate and keep their working relationship strong.

From a project's outset, specialists should clarify their respective roles and responsibilities. Throughout the course of the project they should consult with and advise each other on how they're progressing toward project goals. They should stay up-to-date on each others' deadlines, results, procedures, and operations. They should also work together on the critical task of observing organizational politics to determine any potential effects on the project.

An important tip for both internal and external specialists is at the outset to quickly establish a place among the stakeholders. A specialist who is perceived as a part of the effort and the people involved with the project, is much more likely to be accepted by the employees or performers, their managers, the top-level sponsor or sponsors, and others who will have influence on the process.

Be prepared and be visible. Understand what's required of you before you enter the scene—what skills, knowledge, abilities, and attributes you should possess. You'll want to be a familiar face in the workplace so others will feel comfortable approaching you. It's to your advantage to develop relationships with employees and managers. Remember, established relationships and trust will be of the utmost value later when resistance to change may pose a significant problem.

## Influence of Other Role Players

Other participants in the intervention phase may impact how the intervention specialist works. It's important to know where these other players fit in the process, how they may interact with each other and with you, and what roles they play. It will be useful to learn about:

**Decision makers** who have the final say-so to go ahead with the project, terminate it, completely revise it, or keep it on course; to endorse and oversee follow-up efforts; and to select and direct all resources. Some projects may require a decision-making body to report to a project director. The team would be comprised of individuals from key areas of the organization, including operations and manufacturing, sales and marketing, customer service, and production support. In cases where an external consultant has been contracted to help with the intervention, the consultant should work closely with the project director.

**Performers, employees, or users** who will be at the receiving end of the project—the outcome of the intervention will have a direct impact on these individuals and their jobs. Others who will feel the indirect effect of the intervention while it is in progress or after it ends—included in this group may be employees in other divisions that are not directly involved with the target audience; vendors and suppliers; managers whose responsibilities do not include supervising members of the target audience, resource personnel whose support and assistance—either as subject matter experts or as providers of resource material and equipment—will contribute significantly to the success of the intervention.

# What People Value

It is clear what organizations value in interventions—results that contribute to business goals. It is more difficult to pin down what people want in an intervention. To win acceptance of employees or performers, managers, and sponsors, an intervention should have specific demonstrable value to this group. Here are some indications of what people value, according to experts in the field:

■ *Easy to Learn Solutions*
The performers and others who'll be directly affected by the intervention see it as uncomplicated, understandable, and easy to learn and use on the job. It's very important that this group feels the project is doable—not the intervention specialist, designers, technicians, or subject matter experts.

■ *Simple Solutions*
People are more likely to appreciate an easy-to-use job aid than a complicated software application. If people have an easy time using the intervention material, there's a better chance that most will continue using it on the job and improve their performance. To facilitate on-the-job application, provide plenty of reinforcement from managers and support from technicians.

■ *Best Possible Solutions*
Performers recognize that the intervention is the best available option. They perceive its value for them over past and current solutions. To be sure that they clearly understand the advantages of the intervention, clarify these positive points early in the process and often over the course of the process to reinforce performers' support and cooperation.

■ *Disruption of Work Relationships*
Performers are sensitive to any event or incidence that disrupts the dynamics of their relationships. Unfortunately, many changes in the workplace have an impact on the social environment: people are transferred, laid off, promoted, or reassigned; jobs, titles, expectations, and responsibilities change, which changes the way people define themselves in the workplace; new managers, supervisors, and coworkers bring new perspectives.

■ *A Soap Box for Airing Complaints*
A changing workplace forges new relationships and changes the way people relate to each other. The best way to deal with this is by letting people vent their concerns and discuss their feelings. The best way to handle this and stave off resentments later is to tell people up front what changes will take place and how the social system will change, and provide support and guidance for those in need.

■ *Adaptable Solutions*
Performers and others are more comfortable with solutions that are adaptable to their specific environment or situation. Look for ways to adjust the intervention, while preserving its integral workings and effects. Let people know you're open to altering some features of the project to bring up their level of comfort.

■ *Just-In-Time Solutions*
Performers want solutions that work with the current situation; that is, they want changes that compliment current practice. If past and present operations fit well together, people will be better able to accept the change. Point out how current and future jobs, practices, roles, functions, and goals are the same or similar.

Examples of their administrative and production support include the preparing and distributing of training materials, job aids, guidebooks and manuals, new policy or mission statements, as well as facilitating contact with technicians and other experts who will provide instruction for training and seminars or input in organizational development efforts, incentive and awards programs, change management, motivation initiatives, and strategic planning.

**Organizational contacts** who have a practical need to know about the progress of the intervention or who should be copied on communications at various points in the process.

**Clients, customers, and key stakeholders** who may not be directly involved with the intervention process but who will observe and experience some of its effects.

**The key sponsor from senior management** who has committed organizational support in the form of money and resources and has pledged to work toward the success of the project and toward maintaining its positive effects.

## Types of Interventions

Interventions may be classified according to four main types:

### ■ *Human Resource Development*
This type of intervention is geared specifically toward improving the performance of individual employees. Ways to implement the intervention include training, career development, individual feedback, incentives, and rewards.

### ■ *Organizational Development*
This focuses on improving group and team performance by using team building, organizational design, changes in organizational culture, feedback for groups, incentives, and rewards.

### ■ *Human Resources Management*
This category centers on coaching and managing the performance of both individuals and groups and involves recruiting and staffing efforts. Key areas are leadership, supervision, selection, and succession planning.

### ■ *Environmental Engineering*
This concerns providing performance improvement tools and facilities, such as ergonomics, electronic resources, systems design, environmental design, job aids, and job or organizational design.

## Facts About Intervention

Interventions can be used to solve problems specific to:

- the workplace
- training efforts
- business operations
- performance improvement

Interventions may speak to a number of issues, including:

- employee knowledge and skill levels
- job expectations and feedback
- business processes and time requirements
- tools, resources, and technologies

Interventions may also be designed to concentrate on "transformational issues," such as:

- the leadership of an organization
- the external workplace environment
- the organization's culture
- individual performance
- organizational performance
- the organization's mission and strategies

Or interventions may be used for "transactional" issues, such as:

- business systems and structures
- management practices
- work atmosphere and motivation programs
- individual needs and values
- individual skills and performance
- organizational performance

Interventions can be focused on particular aspects of the business. Some examples include:

*Building the workforce*—selection, hiring, and recruitment efforts.

*Motivating workers*—programs establishing goals, providing incentives, and granting rewards.

*Developing and supplying support for workers*—job aids, training programs, and performance feedback reports.

*Improving the workplace*—better workflow plans and upgraded equipment and greater accessibility to needed information and data.

## Where to Intervene

Interventions may take place on various organizational levels—in an isolated section or throughout dozens of multinational firms with one parent company. The lowest-scale, entry-level intervention is within a unit, department, or division of an organization. Most interventions occur at this point where specific operations and processes may be observed. No other area of the organization is observed or analyzed and only the perceived problems within the unit are addressed.

A step up involves looking at the organization as a whole. Larger issues such as policies, production levels, and product quality may be part of the analysis. Influences outside the organization are not taken into account because the focus is solely on the organization.

# Politics: Separating Fact from Fiction

One of the biggest obstacles to the success or progress of an intervention project is organizational politics. Here are some truths about working in an organization that too often are overlooked or even discounted as untrue. Remember to trust facts and first-hand knowledge over hearsay or the relentless claim that "it's always been this way." Sometimes the conventional wisdom turns out to be unconventionally false and misleading Following are a couple of situational examples:

**Situation:** You're confused about the authority of the manager in the organization and in the intervention process—because you've always held that the best management approach is one in which leadership is shared.

**Reality:** The fact is you'll be happiest working with managers who act like leaders and if you're the project manager for the intervention the organization's management will be happiest if you take control as leader for the project. There's nothing wrong with assuming the responsibilities of making decisions and giving directions, unless those actions are based on inadequate information you need. A smooth implementation of the intervention depends on clearly defined management roles.

**Situation:** You're concerned that the organization is not operating as a true democracy.

**Reality:** This is actually a good sign in many instances. Management by consensus may work in some situations, but by and large most successful for-profit organizations are run by top-down management structures. Most of the time, managers alone will make decisions. In some instances they'll decide after consulting advisors. In a small amount of cases they'll be part of the decision-making process as the member of a team or committee.

**Situation:** You're spending endless hours trying to bring all parties to consensus on an issue.

**Reality:** Who said every individual must agree? Note the fact that all that's required for a consensus is agreement by most of the people involved. What matters is that most people support the decision and believe it is best for the organization or undertaking. If most pledge commitment to supporting the selected intervention and implementing it, there is consensus.

Higher on the scale are interventions to completely change corporate culture. This may involve several organizations and their customers within one network or system, such as a group of corporations whose operations are based on supplier or vendor relationships. The intervention should address concerns about organizational culture, delivery of goods and services, work input processes and results, corporate values, and particularly customer services. Analysis should center on the related organizations—both as individual entities and as they work with each other, the customer base, and current and planned markets.

## Intervention Design and Development

There are various models for designing interventions, most include the following basic steps:

**1. Plan the design project.**
This involves selecting a diverse design team—if desired—according to specifications for covering a range of skills, knowledge, and special expertise. After the selection, planning includes providing the team with an introduction to the design project and an overview of its requirements.

**2. Explain expected results.**
The design team should have an opportunity to carefully examine all available project data to date. The team should have a clear understanding of what the organization expects the design project to deliver. It should have specifications on the scope of the project and all available resources and support.

**3. Set and prioritize requirements.**
The better the quality of the requirements, which form the basis of the intervention, the greater your chances of developing a successful intervention. To make sure you have a solid basis, gather input from a variety of stakeholders, which may include clients, managers, technical experts, and performers.

**4. Decide on the intervention elements.**
The project's designers should use the requirements to determine the components needed to develop a successful intervention. Each component or element should correspond to each requirement, beginning with the most important ones. Each component needs to address specific performance improvement situations.

Designers will find that the process of identifying components will require them to look past obvious elements such as training. They'll do well to consider a wider range of possibilities that may include changes to business operations and incentive programs, among other options.

**5. Identify intervention details.**
Decide on particular activities, events, processes, procedures, and needed resources. Be very specific so that everyone involved will have a clear understanding of the scope of the project and the exact specifications required to develop the intervention.

**6. Plan commitment and approval.**
In this last step of the process it's important to know that final approval of the plan depends on how well it is documented. Mapping it out for the organization's decision makers may seem an arduous task, but it is all-important and deserves careful attention, fine-tuning, and a great deal of revision. This crucial effort will provide all the information decision makers need to decide the future of the project—whether the intervention requires further revision, how it will be developed, or whether it will be dropped.

## Model for Design and Development

A basic model for designing interventions involves gathering needs and context analysis data as well as information on stakeholders' expectations. The next step is to establish requirements for what the intervention should provide and accomplish, what it should cost, and how long it should take. Together these two steps form the basis for the design.

Next, the design team determines components of the intervention, and specifications and plans for each component. The final step is to document and submit the plan for approval.

Here is a step-by-step outline for the process:

**Step 1:** The design team examines the scope and goals of the project and locates available resources.

**Step 2:** The team looks over needs and context analysis data and gathers information on the expectations of all stakeholders—which may include employees or performers and their managers, senior management or clients with ultimate decision-making authority, technical and subject matter experts, labor and union representatives.

**Step 3:** The team then reviews all of the information available, paying special attention to factors that can have a significant negative impact on an intervention—such as, political difficulties, economic problems, and corporate culture issues. If the team decides that these factors do not pose a risk and the other data supports the need for the project, it will decide to go ahead.

**Step 4:** The team uses the analysis data to determine all requirements for what the intervention should do—for example, appeal to both union and management, exceed federal requirements, and be comprehensible to all employees. Other requirements concern what the intervention needs to operate successfully—for example, labor-management cooperation, employee involvement, and productivity assessment. Requirements for resources, time frame, and budget should also be decided.

**Step 5:** The team drafts, revises, and puts requirements in priority order, then begins working to fulfill the top-priority requirements.

**Step 6:** The team identifies components that address the requirements. For each component it determines specifications then drafts corresponding detailed plans setting out goals, work steps, responsibilities, and needed resources.

**Step 7:** The team writes up the final version of the plan and forwards it to top management for approval.

**Step 8:** If the plan is approved, the team begins developing the intervention sufficiently to start implementing it. It develops implementation guidelines and adheres to deadlines for establishing each component of the plan.

# Boost Your Chances for Success

Most people assume that their best efforts will deliver the best results. Unfortunately, that's not always the case. The truth is, if organizational conditions aren't right, even the most finely honed, technologically sound interventions can fail. By following these guidelines, you'll increase your likelihood of success.

**Make sure the intervention** is linked to the most important organizational goals.

**Pick the best time** to start implementing the intervention by avoiding high-activity periods when the organization is obliged to concentrate its best resources and personnel on other demanding projects.

**Garner support from top management**—the kind of support that produces action, not just verbal compliments. A recognized leader within the organization will be a highly effective advocate for the intervention and can help you encourage other senior managers to lend their support.

**Invite employees to contribute** to the intervention and claim some ownership for the intervention. Encourage input during all the phases.

**Stretch support and resources** by tying the intervention to other performance improvement projects within the organization.

**Concentrate only on the one or two projects** you're sure you can handle well. It often takes more effort and discipline to let go of some great ideas and put all your energy toward addressing a few priority needs.

**Don't forget to include the all-important evaluation** step. This is a key part of the any performance improvement project—a solid evaluation process helps you sharpen your intervention and improve your chances for success.

**Keep lines of communication open** to everyone. Stakeholders should hear about the intervention process on a regular basis, so remember to disseminate updates on the details of and reasons for your actions.

**Take note of achievements** throughout the process. As the intervention progresses, stop to congratulate participants and stakeholders at regular intervals. By lauding small accomplishments you can call attention to improvements and bolster those individuals who'll provide long-term support.

**Stay committed,** performance improvement demands a great deal of time. Chart interventions from start to finish, allowing enough time to realize each organizational goal.

**Don't accept** any deadlines that fall before management and other stakeholders have a chance to see the intervention deliver results.

## Development How-tos

After the project receives approval, the work of developing the intervention begins. This phase involves converting specifications of the project into products that can be implemented. These may include instructional manuals, training supplies, job aids, and other materials.

Unlike the project's designers who work on the concept and overall planning, intervention developers engage in hands-on creation of the products needed to implement the intervention. In some cases, particularly if the design is intricate or still in a preliminary stage, designers and developers work together during part of the development process. Other times, when the project is fairly straightforward and specifications are clearly outlined, developers may proceed without the designers' assistance.

Here are some basic steps for the development phase:

1. Put together a development team. Teams work best for both design and development. Select individuals who have the necessary production skills and knowledge to prepare the materials. Remember that although designers are sometimes used in development efforts, it's usually better to assemble a group of production specialists to do this work. If there are many production jobs, consider outsourcing the work.

**2.** Map out the development effort in detail. Make a chart of the specific tasks and resources needed, along with a proposed schedule for starting and finishing each task. Submit these development plans for approval by the client or senior management.

**3.** Make models of the materials and test them. If the production effort will be extensive, and therefore costly, it would be wise to put together some prototypes or drafts of the intervention materials to see how well they'll work—before investing in expensive production and implementation efforts. Examples of prototypes could include a few finished pieces as well as storyboards, scripts, or outlines.

**4.** Test prototypes by submitting them for review by clients, managers, decision makers in the organization, and subject matter experts. You may also decide to run a pilot program in which the target audience has an opportunity to actually use the materials. Remember, the use of these models can provide important feedback to apply in revising the development plan before proceeding to full production.

**5.** Change the development plan based on this kind of feedback and preliminary evaluation efforts. These are enormously valuable steps to take to avoid costly production mistakes. By first testing the material you'll be able to correct weak points in the intervention before producing the materials—and implementing the entire project.

**6.** Once you've taken care of all revisions to the development plan, production may begin. Steps will be taken to gather, put together, and prepare final materials for the intervention.

## Ask the Right Questions to Get the Big Picture

Starting off on the wrong foot can doom the project. Too often designers don't have a clear idea of what key decision makers expect of the project, don't have any background on solutions that were tried in the past, don't have an advocate or sponsor in the organization to support the project, and don't understand that they may not traverse boundaries the organization has placed around what they can do.

To avoid serious mistakes at the outset, intervention designers should seek information on:

- how the organization defines the need for the intervention

- who the organization has designated to be the sponsor for the project

- what the sponsor expects and how he or she will demonstrate a strong commitment to the project

- who else among upper management are stakeholders in the project and what results they expect of the intervention

- what the project will cover and how much time it will take to complete

- who the project will affect and what these people expect of the results

- what kinds of similar interventions have taken place in the organization and what their outcomes were

- what funds and resources are available to support the project

- what kinds of limitations exist

- what other issues—political, financial, cultural—that may impact on the intervention

## Scope of the Project

Ask about the target audience, the effect of the project on job performance, anticipated results with or without the project, location, and materials. Build your specific questions around the following checklist:

☐ How many people will the intervention affect? Of this group, how many will be expected to incorporate the learning or changes directly into their performance?

☐ How many others, aside from those directly affected, must be told that the intervention will be taking place?

# Tips for Selection, Design, and Development

Specialists aim to put together interventions that must meet needs that can be measured, are cost-effective, address the complete problem, and are integrated into the entire organization. Because performance problems may have several underlying causes, performance improvement often calls for combinations of different interventions.

By combining different kinds of interventions that may include training with various forms of support on the job such as job-specific tools, resources, and documentation, you can bolster your chances for success. Add more to your potential for triumph by rallying the support of management; specifically, get managers to participate in the intervention and provide employees with support after it has ended.

Following are some tips for selecting, designing, and developing interventions, based on research by long-standing experts in the field of human performance improvement.

- Get the big picture of the performance problem for use in selecting or designing the intervention by carefully considering all data from the cause analysis phase.

- Make sure intervention designs are based on a thorough understanding of the complete performance improvement process.

- Carefully target the intervention to be sure not only that you've picked the right audience, but that the intervention will produce outcomes worth the organization's investment of time, resources, and staff.

- Seek out a sponsor from upper management who has the authority to commit the required funds and resources to the performance improvement effort.

- Use an interdisciplinary team to design the intervention. Combined expertise is the best strategy for addressing the various performance situations and needed solutions.

- Invite affected employees and managers to contribute to the team. They're most likely to understand how the target audience will benefit from the intervention.

- Make sure the team designs the best—and most cost-effective—solution that meets the requirements of your intervention plan to correct the performance problem.

- For the design, spend time and resources according to the greatest needs and most critical factors involved in solving the performance problem.

- Plan the design with the development and implementation phases in mind—particularly the costs of these phases.

- Incorporate the intervention's various requirements (acquired during the front-end needs analysis) into all design decisions.

- Requirements should address solutions to a problem or need, all stakeholders' expectations regarding ultimate results, the particular process the intervention will involve, the time frame for the project, and the kinds of resources that will be available.

- Use all available data on both design and operational requirements.

- Identify all applicable requirements by gathering input from clients, upper management, subject matter or technical experts, performers and their managers, and any literature or sources that will provide useful information about staffing, technology, equipment, business operations, and strategic goals.

- Select or design interventions that the organization will be able to implement. Don't waste time and money on a design that may be impossible to apply.

- Aim for a long-term, low-cost solution. Use your available resources to create a broad-based, inclusive intervention that will endure over the long term.

- Revise constantly, keeping in mind all subsequent phases of the project. Getting your intervention just right means ongoing testing, trials, changes, feedback, and fine-tuning. Save money in the long run by revising early and often, using as much feedback from all stakeholders.

☐ How does the intervention affect performance—what kinds of jobs and how many will be affected?

☐ What are the expected results of conducting the intervention?

☐ What would happen to performance without the intervention?

☐ If there would be negative results, how extensive would they be? Would it be possible to reverse the effect of such results?

☐ Will the intervention project occur in more than one place? If so, are the sites near one another?

☐ What kinds of equipment and tools are required for the project? Will they be simple or difficult to use?

## Project Resources

You will also want to ask about available resource material and personnel, scheduled deadlines, available funds, needed equipment, procedures for requesting support. Frame your specific questions using this guideline checklist:

☐ Is there a reliable count of how many people are willing to provide support for the project?

☐ What kinds of skills and experience will each person bring to the project? What are their other commitments?

☐ What is the time frame for the project and when are the most important deadlines? What are the possible repercussions of missing any deadlines?

☐ What is the budget? How is the money divided among the phases and tasks? Are there any constraints on the budget or the way funds are planned to be spent?

☐ How much and what kinds of data and information are currently available? Will access to the data be restricted? Have they been checked for accuracy?

☐ What kinds of equipment, tools, and materials are accessible? What amounts of these resources are available for use? What channels must be used to obtain them?

## Project Limitations

You will also need information about restrictions on the use of resource materials and personnel, budget limitations, deadlines, laws and regulations, contracts, cultural issues, and expected reactions from the target audience. Use the following checklist of questions as a guideline for drafting questions tailored to your specific situation:

☐ Will there be constraints on the use of resources and resource personnel?

☐ At what points during the organization's business cycle will key contributors be unable to work on the project? What procedures and channels must be used to ask for their support?

☐ What are the budget constraints for the various cost categories?

☐ What is the schedule for deadlines? Are the dates organized so that tasks and events can be completed in sequence?

☐ Are plans in place for complying with laws, government regulations, and legally binding agreements?

☐ Do contracts and other documents mandate the use of specific language?

☐ Are union employees restricted, under the terms of the union contract, regarding the kind of work they can do, the amount of hours they work, and the amount and kind of compensation they receive?

☐ Is there an affirmative action program in place or any other organized effort requiring representation of specific groups?

☐ Will safety or environmental regulations constrain any project activities?

# Tips for Handling Political Hot Buttons

Political situations in organizations, as elsewhere, have to do with power—who has it, how much of it they have and how it's being used. Knowing how politics and power work in organizations can often make or break an intervention project. Before expending energy, time, and resources be sure to assess the political climate and decide on strategies to deal with any current or potential difficulties. Here are a few approaches you can use to avoid or diffuse power problems.

Build your support base through employee involvement in the project. The strength that exists in numbers really is an effective source of power. The more participants you have in the planning and implementation stages, the more power you'll have. Some examples of employee involvement include total quality management efforts, self-managed work teams, and participative management.

**Know what kind of organization** you're working with and how power is used. Is the focus on controlling the flow of information or making sure the information is correct and timely? Is the decision-making focused on identifying problems and opportunities for improvement? Or is it dependent on intuition and feelings, and the views of the organization's visionary leaders?

**Understand that knowledge is power** and make every effort to gather as much information as you can about the company's industry, business operation, background, strategic goals, mission, and plans for the future.

**Disarm your opponents.** The easiest way to disperse their power is by facing the problem. Bring it out in the open and make sure people get a chance to discuss what's bothering them. Address their complaints and make it clear that you recognize their discomfort. The best way to ease their fear is with simple, straightforward facts about what will happen during the changes.

**Use power in subtle ways.** A great show of it will threaten people. The best way to bring about change is in increments with each effort tailored to a specific improvement that will clearly benefit the target audience.

**Join forces with others in the organization** who have power. These partnerships and close working relationships are most effective with managers who have direct influence on the performers who will be using the changes on the job.

**Build credits you can use later**. If you attend to projects that senior managers perceive as most important, you may be able to begin working on your own ideas and programs for improvement.

**Capitalize on your successes** and take advantage of the timing. After a winning intervention, follow up quickly with one that may not be as appealing. This is the best approach under the circumstances. Sometimes, you've got to help implement unpopular changes. If you, and your target audience, don't have a choice it may be best to get on with the required changes as fast as possible during a time when most people are feeling positive about change in general.

**Present data and research** to diffuse potentially volatile occurrences. Facts are always an effective antidote to heated arguments, angry statements by a few powerful individuals, and other situations in which emotions run high.

**Use trials and pilot programs** as a nonthreatening way to ease people into the changes. This gives others a sense of ownership, control, and participation in the decision to go ahead with the final intervention.

**Stay in tune to the feelings and attitudes** of important players. Throughout the intervention maintain regular communication with these people, keep them informed of any changes and developments, and let them know that you're aware and interested in their responses and feedback.

**Try to take it one step at a time.** Nurture burgeoning acceptance among both managers and performers by introducing changes incrementally. Small, well-paced steps will help to ease their fears.

☐ Are there corporate procedures in place that dictate conduct regarding: ways to contact individuals; how to lead meetings, when to schedule them, where to hold them; how to request information; how to disseminate printed matter?

☐ What cultural factors must be addressed—what customs or preferences regarding: the way people dress, the way they speak and the languages they use, how groups and individuals interact with each other, the schedule and site for project activities that involve interaction, the way results of the project should be presented?

☐ What are the limitations on decisions about the intervention project? Which, if any, decisions have been made? Are there any acceptable alternatives or substitutes for these decisions?

☐ What specifications does the decision-making process require?

☐ How are people expected to respond to the project? Are they concerned about losing status, or losing the jobs themselves? Have there been similar projects in the past that may have created problems for some people?

## Assisting With Implementation Tasks

Once an intervention has been selected, intervention specialists may assist the change manager with helping performers, managers, process owners, and other stakeholders to prepare to implement the intervention. Some tasks include:

● assessing the organization's efforts to deal with the causes of the performance gap

● developing solutions and strategies to address those causes

● evaluating organizational changes—both internal and external—that could have an impact on the implementation

● specifying and stressing each way the intervention can help the organization fulfill its needs, determine its goals and objectives, and carry out its mission

● seeking out the organization's finest resources and talent to ensure a successful intervention

## Monitoring the Intervention

During the implementation, HPI professionals and intervention specialists regularly track the process to keep it focused on achieving the planned results. They look carefully for:

● Indications that the intervention is having an impact on what's causing the performance gaps.

● Improvements that can be measured.

● Evidence that the stakeholders have established ownership in the intervention, and whether that ownership should be increased.

● Signs that organizational as well as external changes—such as changes in business operations, work environment, staffing and technology, and vendor relationships—are having an impact on the intervention.

## Competencies

Effecting smooth implementation and seamless transitions during interventions requires the intervention specialist to possess the following competencies:

● deciding which actions the organization should take in dealing with current and future causes of performance gaps

● navigating the organizational channels and networks and getting messages through—and building those alliances and networks to boost productivity and performance

● working with others to meet work, group, and individual goals

- understanding the various interactions among individuals and groups and the outcomes of those interactions

- helping others such as employees and their managers, process owners, and stakeholders to gain new perspectives on the intervention

## Dealing With Obstacles

Some potential impediments to putting the intervention in place include concerns that the activity is too difficult to understand or do, that individual contributions won't be visible, that results won't be apparent and may be delayed, that small risk-free trials won't be possible, or that current values and practices won't be addressed. The best way to tackle these obstacles is to identify each and develop one or more solutions specific to the concern or problem. Following are several examples of potential problems and how to handle them:

### ■ *Too Difficult to Understand*

If a project-related task or activity is too difficult to comprehend, pinpoint what elements are causing the difficulty and try to simplify them. Use an introduction that gives a broad overview of the project. Make your points clearer by using visuals and concrete examples that are familiar to most people. Enlist the aid of someone in the group who knows how people in the target audience talk about things, the terminology they use, their views and attitudes.

### ■ *Takes Too Much Energy and Effort*

If people feel they're required to expend too much energy and effort on the activity, show them—don't just tell them—that what they're being asked to do requires only a reasonable amount of work. Break each task down into simple steps, simplify the task itself, divide one task among several participants, or use equipment and job aids.

### ■ *Contributions Unrecognized*

If individuals are concerned that the organization won't know about their contribution or participation, become their publicity agent and announce the names of everyone who was involved in the intervention. You may also recast tasks to make them visible or add tasks that are more appropriate for public display.

### ■ *Insufficient Rewards*

If people are concerned that the rewards are too slight, change the current recognition system or institute one that has the group's approval. Send an organizationwide announcement detailing the significance and value of the task. Or, change the task to make it more fulfilling.

### ■ *Results Take Too Long*

If the concern is about waiting a long time for the outcome, measure results during the process and explain their significance. Or, focus on the rewarding aspects of the activity or task—and be sure to offer a great deal of reinforcement and assurance.

### ■ *Participation Is Limited*

If they feel they can only participate by becoming involved in all aspects of the project rather than just one or two, reassure them that they're free to try a few components of the task or activity. Or, invite a group of people, who are particularly supportive of the project, to test it.

## Managing Change

An effective intervention specialist must also be skilled in managing change. The reason for this is that performance improvement interventions disrupt the status quo because they usually require changes that have significant impact on the way the organization and the individual work. If these changes aren't handled carefully, the implementation may not succeed.

Expect many in the workforce to be reluctant to change, especially if the changes will directly affect performance. You can overcome this obstacle by soliciting help from other HPI professionals, senior management, and employees to enable the workforce to move beyond resisting to accepting the changes. To gain further insight on the change manager's role for HPI, refer to *Info-line* No. 9715, "The Role of the Performance Change Manager."

One way the intervention specialist can assist in the change management process is to coordinate the intervention project. This is a plan or contract detailing how the change process is critical to the success of the intervention. Each plan should include:

- a statement of goals
- a corresponding statement of objectives
- a list of project limitations and restrictions
- a list of anticipated obstacles and problems
- a chart of tasks to be accomplished
- an explanation of key jobs and functions
- the relationships between key players

## Following Up

Postintervention information can be a valuable resource for fine-tuning future efforts and for avoiding potentially costly mistakes. The data you collect now, to help you assess both your errors and achievements, will help you market your services later. Here are some tips for collecting information and using it to your advantage.

1. Gather facts and details about the success of the intervention from line managers and other decision makers who had hands-on involvement with the project. Use their input as a benchmark for gauging their satisfaction with the performance improvement project.

2. If you receive positive feedback, take advantage of it. Request that those internal customers contact the company newsletter to publish an article about your services.

3. Feature these satisfied clients at your next presentation and invite them to offer testimonials about your services.

4. Suggest that they talk with other line managers and decision makers about the products and services you provide.

5. Review data on unsuccessful projects to see if the intervention did not fit the performance problem, to learn from any errors and avoid similar ones later, and to determine whether your staff requires training to improve their skills.

# References & Resources

## Articles

Carr, C., and L. Totzke. "The Long and Winding Path from Instructional Technology to Performance Technology." *Performance & Instruction*, August 1995, pp. 4-8.

Clark, R.C. "Hang Up Your Training Hat." *Training & Development*, September 1994, pp. 61-65.

Elliot, P. "Power-Charging People's Performance." *Training & Development* December 1996, pp. 46-49.

Esque, T.J. "Eventful Interventions." *Performance Improvement*, October 1996, pp. 30-32.

Gephart, M.A. "The Road to High Performance." *Training & Development*, June 1995, pp. 30-38.

Middlebrook, J.F. "How To Manage Individual Performance." *Training & Development*, September 1996, pp. 45-48.

Rummler, G. "In Search of the Holy Performance Grail." *Training & Development*, April 1996, pp. 26-32.

Smalley, K., et al. "Strategic Planning: From Training to Performance Technology Within Three Years." *Performance Improvement Quarterly*, vol. 8, no. 2 (1995), pp. 114-124.

Sorohan, E.G. "The Performance Consultant at Work." *Training & Development,* March 1996, pp. 35-38.

Spitzer, D.R. "Ensuring Successful Performance Improvement Interventions." *Performance Improvement*, October 1996, pp. 26-27.

———. "What to Avoid When Shifting From Training to Performance Consulting." *Training Director's Forum Newsletter,* March 1996, pp. 1-3.

## Books

Argyris, C. I*ntervention Theory and Method.* Reading, Massachusetts: Addison-Wesley, 1970.

ASTD. *Introduction to Performance: A Primer for Trainers.* Alexandria, Virginia: American Society for Training & Development, 1996.

Barger, N., and L. Kirby. *The Challenge of Change in Organizations: Helping Employees Thrive in the New Frontier.* North Carolina: Davies-Black Publishing, 1995.

Bassi, L.J., et al. *The ASTD Training Data Book.* Alexandria, Virginia: American Society for Training & Development, 1996.

Bennis, W., and B. Nanus. *Leaders: The Strategies for Taking Charge.* New York: Harper & Row, 1985.

Block, P. *Flawless Consulting: A Guide to Getting Your Expertise Used.* San Diego, California: University Associates, 1981.

Brinkerhoff, R.O., and S.J. Gill. *The Learning Alliance.* San Francisco: Jossey-Bass, 1994.

Craig, R.L. *The ASTD Training & Development Handbook: A Guide to Human Resource Development (4th ed.).* Alexandria, Virginia: American Society for Training & Development, 1996.

Dubois, D.D. *Competency-Based Performance Improvement.* Amherst, Massachusetts: HRD Press, 1995.

Golembiewski, R. *Handbook of Organizational Consultation.* New York: Marcel Dekker, Inc., 1993.

Gouilart, F., and J. Kelly. *Transforming the Organization: Reframing Corporate Direction, Restructuring the Company, Revitalizing the Enterprise, Renewing People.* New York: McGraw-Hill, 1995.

Holtz, H. *How to Succeed as an Independent Consultant (3rd ed.).* New York: Wiley, 1993.

Kaufman, R. *Strategic Planning: An Organizational Guide.* Newbury Park, California: Sage Publications, 1992.

Kaufman, R., et al. *The Practitioner's Handbook on Organization and Human Performance Improvement.* San Diego, California: University Associates/Pfeiffer and Company, 1995.

Rothwell, W.J. *ASTD Models for Human Performance Improvement.* Alexandria, Virginia: American Society for Training & Development, 1996.

Rothwell, W.J., et al. *Practicing Organization Development: A Guide for Consultants.* San Diego, California: Pfeiffer & Co., 1995.

Rothwell, W., and H. Kazanas. *Human Resource Development: A Strategic Approach.* Amherst, Massachusetts: HRD Press, 1994.

Rummler, G., and A. Brache. *Improving Performance: How to Manage the White Space on the Organization Chart.* San Francisco: Jossey-Bass, 1990.

Stolovich, H.D., and E.J. Keeps. *Handbook of Human Performance Technology: A Comprehensive Guide for Analyzing and Solving Performance Problems in Organizations.* San Francisco: Jossey-Bass, 1992.

Swanson, R.A. *Analysis for Improving Performance: Tools for Diagnosing Organizations & Documenting Workplace Expertise.* San Francisco: Berrett-Koehler Publishers, 1994.

# Intervention Specialist Competencies Assessment Checklist

Below are listed the required competencies and enabling outputs for the role of intervention specialist as outlined in *ASTD Models for Human Performance Improvement*. Read each entry and assess your rate of competency and ability to produce enabling outputs as: **satisfactory, needs improvement, or unsatisfactory.** In the space provided list the ways you plan to improve your competency level for the particular area—examples may include becoming active in professional associations, reading journals and periodicals in the field, working on projects with others, and observing and emulating role models.

## I. Performance Information Interpretation Skills

☐ Find useful meaning from the performance analysis results and help performers, their managers, process owners, and other stakeholders also find meaning.

Rate: _____

Rate your ability to produce enabling outputs:

☐ Present written or oral briefings to all stakeholders about the results of the performance or cause analyses:

_____

_____

_____

☐ Draw useful information from the analyses:

_____

_____

_____

☐ I will improve my performance information interpretation skills by taking the following actions:

_____

_____

_____

## II. Intervention Selection Skills

☐ Select HPI interventions that address root causes of performance gaps rather than just symptoms or side effects.

Rate: _____

Rate your ability to produce enabling outputs:

☐ Apply approaches for choosing appropriate HPI strategies to close gaps.

☐ I will improve my intervention selection skills by taking the following actions:

_____

_____

_____

## III. Performance Change Interpretation Skills

☐ Forecast and analyze the effects of interventions and their consequences.

Rate: _____

Rate your ability to produce enabling outputs:

☐ Produce written and oral briefings to stakeholders about the expected impact of changes or interventions on processes, individuals, or the organization.

☐ Use problem-solving activities to lead stakeholders to identify or anticipate the impact of an intervention on processes, individuals, or the organization.

## Job Aid

☐ I will improve my performance change interpretation skills by taking the following actions:

_____

_____

_____

## IV. Ability to Assess Relationships Among Interventions

☐ Examine the effects of multiple interventions on parts of an organization and on the organization's interactions with customers, suppliers, distributors, and employees.

Rate: _____

Rate your ability to produce enabling outputs:

☐ Produce written and oral briefings to stakeholders about the expected impact of multiple interventions on processes, individuals, or the organization.

☐ Use problem-solving activities to lead stakeholders to identify or anticipate the impact of multiple interventions on processes, individuals, or the organization.

☐ I will improve my ability to assess relationships among interventions by taking the following actions:

_____

_____

_____

## V. Ability to Identify Critical Business Issues and Changes

☐ Identify the key business issues and apply this information during the intervention's implementation.

Rate: _____

Rate your ability to produce enabling outputs:

☐ Produce organizational and process analyses, individual assessments, white papers on HPI strategies, oral and written briefings on possible intervention strategies, customer satisfaction information and survey results.

☐ I will improve my ability to identify critical business issues and changes by taking the following actions:

_____

_____

_____

## VI. Goal Implementation Skills

☐ Ensure that goals are converted into actions to close existing or pending performance gaps.

Rate: _____

☐ Get results despite conflicting priorities, lack of resources, or ambiguity.

Rate: _____

Rate your ability to produce enabling outputs:

☐ Produce written or oral HPI goals and intervention performance objectives.

☐ Facilitate performance objectives.

☐ I will improve my goal implementation skills by taking the following actions:

_____

_____

_____

*The material appearing on this page is not covered by copyright and may be reproduced at will.*

# The Role of the Performance Change Manager

The Role of the Performance
Change Manager

Issue 9715

# The Role of the Performanc Change Manager

**AUTHOR:**

**Deborah Koehle**

Deborah A. F. Koehle is an editor with ASTD, responsible for the production of *National Report on Human Resources* and *Performance in Practice*. She is also a graduate student at Johns Hopkins University studying applied behavioral science, with a concentration in organization development.

**Editor**
Cat Sharpe

**Associate Editor**
Patrick McHugh

**Designer**
Steven M. Blackwood

**Copy Editor**
Kay Larson

**ASTD Internal Consultant**
Dr. Walter Gray

# The Role of the Change Manager

This is the third *Info-line* in a series of four looking at the roles involved in the Human Performance Improvement Process. The HPI process involves four roles—analyst, intervention specialist, change manager, and evaluator. The roles may be filled by one person or several people. The first four steps in the process—analysis, intervention, implementation, and change management—can happen concurrently or sequentially. For example, while analysis of the performance problem is being conducted, the change manager can be assessing organizational readiness and mapping out communication channels and networks. The last step, evaluation and measurement, begins after implementation of the interventions.

The first two *Info-lines* in this series define the roles of analyst and intervention specialist. We will assume that at this point in the HPI process, performance and cause analyses have been performed and interventions have been selected. Now, it's time for the change manager to step in.

As defined by William Rothwell in *ASTD Models for Human Performance Improvement,* change managers are responsible for implementation and change management (see the following two pages). Change managers ensure that interventions are implemented in ways consistent with desired results and they help individuals and groups achieve those desired results in healthy ways.

During the implementation and change management process, the change manager will use his or her knowledge of group dynamics and skills in process consultation and facilitation to help organizational members adjust to the change, stay on course, and deal with roadblocks along the way. The change manager will also be responsible for developing communication plans that explain the change and keep everyone up-to-date on the progress of the change.

The five competencies required of the change manager are:

1. Change impetus skills.

2. Communication channel, informal network, and alliance understanding.

3. Group dynamics process understanding.

4. Process consultation skills.

5. Facilitation skills.

This *Info-line* will explore each of these competencies in terms of how the change manager uses these skills and understandings to successfully implement and manage change.

## Change Impetus Skills

As stated before, change management can begin concurrently with analysis and/or intervention selection, or after these steps. Before implementation begins, a change strategy must be chosen. Gathering data about the time needed, the extent of the change, and the change targets will guide the development of the change management plan. Before you write your plan, you'll want to keep in mind the following principle of change: **Change in any part of the organization affects other parts of the organization.** When people initiate change, it is viewed as good, needed, and valuable. When change is forced on people, the change is generally met with resistance. Remember the following:

- People need physical, psychological, and social predictability.

- People also need variety, chances to grow, breaks in routine, and so forth.

- Plan your changes in a way that doesn't threaten security but allows opportunity for growth.

# Outputs Associated with Change Management

| Role | Competencies | Enabling Outputs | |
|---|---|---|---|
| **Change Manager—** ensures that interventions are implemented in ways consistent with desired results and that they help individuals and groups achieve results. | **Change Impetus Skills** —determining what the organization should do to address the cause(s) of a human performance gap at present and in the future. | • a convincing case made for the need for change<br><br>• organizational sponsorship identified and secured<br><br>• evidence of support obtained through commitment of resources<br><br>• designs/action plans for introducing<br><br>• designs/action plans for reducing resistance to interventions<br><br>• recommendations to management about management's role in introducing and consolidating change<br><br>• recommendations to workers about their role in introducing and consolidating change | • performance improvement interventions effectively monitored with participants and stakeholders<br><br>• effective interpersonal interactions among participants and stakeholders of interventions<br><br>• tracking systems to compare actual and ideal performance and progress toward narrowing or closing performance gaps, or realizing performance opportunities as the intervention is implemented<br><br>• oral and/or written agreements among most or all stakeholders about the results desired from the intervention<br><br>• measurable financial or nonfinancial objectives to be achieved during and after implementation of the intervention(s) |
| | **Communication Channel, Informal Network, and Alliance Understanding**—knowing how communication moves through an organization by various channels, networks, and alliances; building such channels, networks and alliances to achieve improvements in productivity and performance. | • communication plans established to keep participants in change and stakeholders of change informed about the progress of the human performance improvement intervention. | |

| Competencies | Enabling Outputs |
|---|---|
| **Group Dynamics Process Understanding** — understanding how groups function; influencing people so that group, work, and individual needs are addressed. | • groups successfully observed<br><br>• plans for influencing groups based on knowledge of small group development theory |
| **Process Consultation Skills**—observing individuals and groups for their interactions and the effects of their interactions with others. | • group process observation forms<br><br>• descriptions to group members and individuals about the effects of their behavior on a group or on individuals |
| **Facilitation Skills**—helping performers, performers' managers, process owners, and stakeholders discover new insights. | • plans for facilitating group discussions<br><br>• plans for facilitating individual or group decision making and problem solving |

*Adapted from William Rothwell,* ASTD Models for Human Performance Improvement, *1996.*

Ways to ensure that your plan takes into consideration these principles is to provide enough lead time to prepare for change. You can accomplish this in the following ways:

- Involve employees in implementation.

- Expect resistance.

- Expect that the amount of time it takes for change to be accepted will vary.

- Identify networks that can help facilitate bringing about the change.

- Communicate clearly.

- Reward appropriately.

The change management plan provides the road map that both the change manager and the organization can use as a guide. The plan details problems faced by an organization, what change is required to address those problems, how the change will be instituted, and what values and behaviors are needed to bring about the change.

Explaining what has happened in the past helps justify the need for change and gives historical perspective. It also creates a way to acknowledge where the organization has been and allows the change management plan to serve as a bridge to show where the organization is going in the future.

The most successful change management plans:

- establish the need for the change
- involve people
- sustain commitment

The plan details how the needed changes will affect the worker (the performer level), the workplace (the organizational level), and the work (the process level). The plan also needs to contain a great deal of information, including who is sponsoring the change, what resources will be committed to the change effort, what role managers and employees will play, what behaviors will be expected, how resistance will be reduced, and how the process will be tracked and measured.

## Making a Case for Change

Working on the assumption that analyses and intervention selection have already occurred, we can also assume that the need for the change has already been determined. It is up to the change manager to present the need for change in a persuasive and convincing way. As people are generally reluctant to change, employees are not likely to embrace change for reasons they don't find convincing.

One way to make a convincing argument is to review what was discovered in the analyses. Explain where the company is, where it needs to go, and why. Be sure employees understand how market forces and customer demands are affecting the organization. One piece of information that can prove a powerful influence on employees is explaining the consequences for the company if nothing changes and these performance gaps are not filled.

Because "doing nothing" is always an option, employees need a full understanding of what maintaining the status quo will mean. This is known as pain management, which means information given to employees about the need for change must lead employees to believe that the price for the status quo is significantly higher than the price of change. Without a compelling need for change, organizations will not change.

When explaining to employees the gaps between where the company is and where it needs to be, be honest about the challenges the employees and the company will face in trying to eliminate those gaps. Explain how the gaps will be closed, in what order, and by whom. This process of moving employees toward the desired state is known as *remedy selling*. Operational goals and how success in achieving those goals will be measured must be clearly defined.

The change manager is responsible for identifying and securing organizational sponsorship, and since the sponsor supports the project by committing necessary resources. This is one risk factor in the successful implementation of the plan. Employees will be assessing the seriousness of the project based on a number of criteria, including the strength of the commitment among those sponsoring the change. Assigning the proper amount of people, time, and money communicates management's seriousness about the need to change.

## Managing Resistance

In planning how to deal with resistance, the change manager will want to look at a number of things. First, assess the organization's overall readiness for change and based on the results, plan how to lessen resistance. A force-field analysis is one way to assess what forces within the organization will impact the attempt to introduce change.

Force-field analysis recognizes two types of forces: driving and restraining. Driving forces are ones that will help you implement the change, while restraining forces are the ones that will get in the way of the change. Since forces are defined based on their positive or negative affect regarding the change, what may appear as a driving force might instead be a restraining force. For example, while incentive systems are generally regarded as a positive, if the existing system is not reinforcing the new behaviors, it becomes a restraining force.

The force-field analysis will ensure three things:

1. You haven't overlooked any areas.

2. You know what forces to take advantage of.

3. You have time to develop other strategies if the analysis reveals areas you hadn't considered previously.

Once the driving and restraining forces are known, strategies can be developed to either take advantage of drivers or reduce the impact of restrainers. By either increasing driving forces or reducing restraining forces, you move the current status quo in the direction of the wanted change. Because systems move toward equilibrium, try to reduce restraining forces rather than increasing driving forces because an increase in driving forces results in an increase in restraining forces.

Your plan for reducing resistance will need to take into account the time necessary for both the people and the organization to react to the change. It will also need to acknowledge the reality that while there is a need to allow time for adjustment, there is still work that needs to be done.

## Learning to Accept Change

While there are a number of change models, they all deal with the process of moving from one reality to another. The process begins with an ending, moves to a transition period, and then to a new beginning. While people generally tend to dislike change because of the disruptions it causes, change is necessary for growth and your plan will need to address ways in which employees can work through each of these stages, especially the transition phase, which can often be a frightening period of unknowns.

A common change model defines the movement through change in terms of *unfreezing—changing—refreezing*.

■ *Unfreezing*
During this stage, the corporate climate begins to change by creating the need to relearn behaviors and/or attitudes. During this phase of change, it is important that a safety net be in place that allows employees the opportunity to recognize the good and bad about the past as the first step in preparing to let go and move forward.

■ *Changing*
During this phase, employees will be looking for guidance on how to use the expected new behaviors. The leadership provides that guidance by modeling the new behaviors and attitudes.

■ *Refreezing*
This phase brings the stabilization of the change, as employees begin to test new behaviors and attitudes. If the behaviors and attitudes are accepted, employees internalize them and begin to take ownership of them.

Another change model defines change acceptance in terms of stages: *denial, resistance, exploration, and commitment*. The change grid (see Figure 1, on the next page) shows how employees progress through the change process. The two axes define the four stages. The horizontal axis begins on the left with a focus on the past and moves to the right, where the focus begins to be the future. The vertical axis has the focus on the external/environment at the top and the internal/self at the bottom.

■ *Denial Phase*
During this phase, employees become aware of the need for change but refuse to deal with the

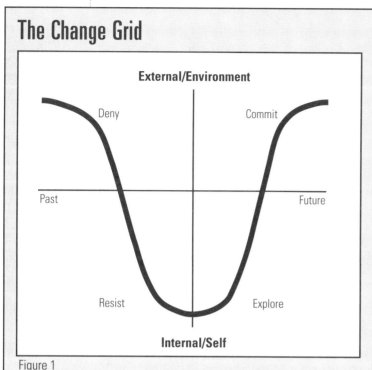

## The Change Grid

Figure 1

*Reprinted from "Changing the Work Culture" by Irwin Rubin and Robert Inguatiato,* Training & Development, *July 1991.*

change, acting as if nothing has changed at all. This phase can drag out, especially if the organization wrongly interprets employees' lack of response to change as acceptance.

#### ■ Resistance Phase
This occurs as employees move through denial and confront their emotions about having to break with the past. This is a time when employees are deciding whether or not they like the changes. Resistant employees need to be able to express negative feelings. Sharing those feelings with others is important as it make employees realize they are not alone. This is a time when the change manager needs to allow employees to safely air their feelings by listening objectively and expressing genuine empathy.

#### ■ Exploration Phase
As employees begin to work through resistance, exploration of what the future will be begins. Employees are preparing themselves for dealing with the change. While this can be a phase of great energy, it can also be a chaotic time as employees search for ways to incorporate the new behaviors. In order to begin accepting the changes, employ-

ees need to fully understand the details of what the change entails. They begin to experiment with new behaviors, attempting to implement them into their work life.

#### ■ Commitment Phase
Finally, as employees find new ways to behave, and see those behaviors rewarded, they move toward commitment. At this point, employees have adopted the change as their own.

In yet another model, seven phases of change are outline as follows:

1. Destabilizing and losing focus.
2. Minimizing the impact.
3. Questioning self-worth.
4. Letting go of the past.
5. Testing the new situation.
6. Searching for meaning.
7. Integrating the experience.

Figure 2, on the next page shows how morale is affected as employees move toward change acceptance.

While each of these models defines the stages differently, one can easily see the similarities between them. In each case, the proponents agree that people move through different stages before accepting change. Both employees and organizations move through these phases. How quickly they are able to move depends on how well the change manager prepares and assists them. One way to provide assistance is to give employees opportunities to come together as a means of giving each other support.

Employees will also need to have time for reflection, which will allow them to consider what is happening and put it in perspective. Consider the value of having forums where the new values and behaviors are discussed and employees give examples of them in action. At these forums, acknowledge that the change process can be difficult and allow employees to share thoughts and emotions. Be willing to confront issues that are raised at the forums and pledge to work to get those issues resolved. Explore ways employees can celebrate success and focus on current accomplishments.

## Getting Commitment

The details of the change management plan should spell out how employees will be personally involved in the change, as involvement is one way to foster commitment to the change. While the change plan lays out where the organization needs to go and what the organization will do as a whole to get there, employees will need to decide how the work processes are redesigned to meet changing needs. This involvement allows employees to increase learning and problem-solving skills. The effort to redesign work also provides employees with opportunities to work through the feelings and emotions that are part of adapting to change.

Other things to keep in mind when initiating change include some of the following:

### ■ *What is going on in the organization?*
Another way to gain commitment is look at what is going on in the organization at a particular time and develop incentives that will make sense to the people in the organization. Commitment to change will increase when the change agenda appeals to employee emotions, generates enthusiasm, paints a picture of what the end state will look like, and provides options that allow different groups within the organization to implement the change in the way that works best for them.

### ■ *Keep Employees Up-to-date*
Other ways to increase involvement include keeping employees up-to-date on how the change effort is progressing, responding to employee feedback, mirroring the new behaviors yourself, allowing employees to make decisions and supporting those decisions, and rewarding employees appropriately.

### ■ *Reward Systems*
Looking at the reward systems is particularly important. Have they been changed to reflect the desired new behaviors and attitudes? It's been said, "What gets rewarded gets done." While the plan may be pushing employees toward new behaviors, if incentive systems are still rewarding old behavior, the attempt to bring about change

will fail. Properly designed reward systems communicate the organization's seriousness about the change and can provide a powerful incentive for employees to take a closer look at how the change can benefit them. The change manager works with the organization to ensure there are intrinsic and extrinsic incentives that will help make the change more attractive and also help make the change take hold.

### ■ *How Will Interventions Be Monitored?*
Finally, the plan will need to define how interventions will be monitored. Ways of tracking performance against financial or nonfinancial measures will provide everyone with a scorecard of how the interventions are working in closing performance gaps.

Because the overall success of the change process depends on the support of managers at all levels of the organization, the change management plan needs their support. Beginning with the top level, use the drafting of the plan as a way to achieve buy in and support. As the plan moves down the organization, employees at every level can fill in the details of how they will contribute to bringing about the needed change.

The plan needs to be flexible in order to meet the needs at each different level. It also needs flexibility so that it can be refined if necessary as implementation progresses.

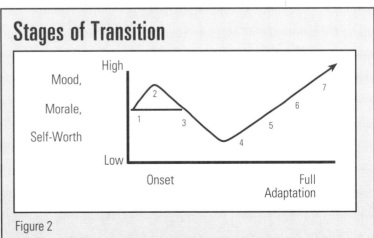

## Stages of Transition

Figure 2

*Reprinted from* Training & Development Journal, *"People in Transition," by J.D. Adams and S.A. Spencer, October 1988.*

## Communication Audit

One way the change manager can help facilitate change acceptance is by having a thorough knowledge of how communication moves through the organization. One way to achieve that understanding is by conducting a communication audit. The communication audit will reveal where communication breakdowns are occurring. It will also note how the formal communication media is received. Such an audit generally consists of information interviews, focus groups, a survey, policy and procedures review, and operations observation. Particular attention needs to be paid to the informal communication networks, which can facilitate or sabotage change efforts.

The information interviews and focus groups will help you begin to understand the communications environment. They will help you define what types of questions should be asked in the survey. Questions for information interviews and focus groups cover topics such as:

- what messages are being received

- message credibility

# Process Consultation Interventions

When serving as a process consultant, the change manager needs to ensure that the group moves successfully toward the completion of its task. To achieve successful group interaction and task accomplishment may require interventions. Examples of types and kinds of interventions are listed in the matrix below.

| Focus | Cognitive | Activities/Skills | Behavior Description | Emotional/ Reflective | Interpretive |
|---|---|---|---|---|---|
| Group | "The group seems to be behind in its completion schedule." | "Let me suggest a decision-making activity that I think you will find helpful." | "You [the group] seem to be interrupting one another in a frantic attempt to influence the outcome." | "Members are sitting on a lot of anger because you didn't influence the decision." | "The group's bitterness over past failures leads me to wonder if you are afraid to become successful." |
| Interpersonal | "You might both consider looking at what you have in common." | "Let me suggest that each of you write a letter to each describing the conflict." | "The two of you are constantly supporting and protecting each other, | but when it is pointed out, you both deny it and become angry and embarrassed." | "...Is it possible that the two of you are fearful of competing with each other?" |
| Individual | "Tim, here is a book on the subject you might consider reading." | "Anne, why don't you take some time right now and record your thoughts and feelings in your journal." | "Whenever the group is ready to make a decision, you seem to bring up another alternative." | "It is clear that you have a great deal of affection for John but are reluctant to talk about it publicly." | "Judy, I wonder if your silence expresses anger at group members for not checking in with you?" |

*Reprinted with permission from* Intervention Skills Process Consultation for Small Groups and Teams *by W. Brendan Reddy, Ph.D., Jossey-Bass/Pfeiffer, 1994.*

- how the leadership is perceived (i.e., do they walk the talk?)

- how information moves through the organization, the quality and quantity of information provided

- the preferred sources of information compared to the actual sources

- what forms of media are preferred for different types of messages

Based on information gathered during the interviews and focus groups, the survey is designed and pretested. In addition to gathering data on the communications environment, you'll want to ask demographic questions such as length of service and work location in order to determine if any particular employee group or area falls outside the norm.

Where demographics indicate a problem, additional communication resources can be allocated. Where demographics indicate an above average communications environment, steps can be taken to learn what is at work and whether any useful ideas can be borrowed for use in other areas of the organization.

Defining informal communication networks can be achieved by performing a network analysis. Generally, there are six types of informal networks:

### ■ *Advice Networks*
These are networks used to solve problems.

### ■ *Trust Networks*
These networks are those where sensitive information is shared.

### ■ *Communication Networks*
These networks are used for discussing work-related matters.

### ■ *Information Networks*
These networks are composed of those who share information with each other, and are where to focus when there is a need to transform technical systems.

### ■ *Influence Networks*
These focus on the political side of the organization, and can be used to change the distribution of power within the organization.

### ■ *Affect Networks*
These networks are those of friendships within the organization, and are closely connected to the corporate culture. If there is a high degree of political uncertainty in an organization, it is nearly impossible to address technical or cultural issues. This makes it all the more imperative that the political players are brought into the change process early and are supportive of it.

During the network analysis, questions to ask include the following:

- Whom do you trust?

- Whom do you talk to for work advice?

- Whom do you go to when you need a problem solved?

- Whom do you go to when you want information about what's going on in the company?

Because trust is such an important element to both change management and open communication, valuable information might be gained by asking, "Whom don't you trust?" In your audit, you will want to determine what the trust level is within the organization. Employees will need to feel a high degree of trust in order to move through the change acceptance stages. Attempts to introduce change into organizations with serious trust problems are likely to fail. If your communication audit finds trust problems, increasing the level of trust will need to be one of the first steps in your change management plan.

Change managers can use informal networks to advance the change agenda by helping bring together groups to serve as teams or task forces in a way that takes advantage of new and old alliances.

Based on the results a completed audit, a formal change communication plan can be developed. The plan should: define objectives, identify the audience, define the key messages, determine the media and timing for delivering the messages, and define what feedback mechanisms will be used to evaluate how the message is being received.

## Feedback Mechanisms

Properly installed feedback mechanisms will ensure that communication flows up from employees to management. Ensuring that communication moves laterally is equally challenging, especially since many organizations are vertically aligned, which discourages information sharing across departmental lines. One way to increase lateral communication is to form cross-functional teams that bring together diverse organizational groups. As the individual team members work together to achieve a common goal, relationships are established and information sharing begins.

The importance of feedback cannot be over emphasized. It is an often overlooked part of the communication process. Without quantifiable feedback mechanisms it is impossible to know for sure how the message is being received. The lack of valid feedback data can limit your ability to ensure the correct messages are being received. Feedback data provides you the chance to know if messages aren't clear and to refine those messages to increase understanding. The process of sending the messages, responding to feedback, clarifying the message, and sending it again must be

repeated continuously, as repetition is an effective method of message reinforcement. This process needs to be addressed in both the formal and informal communication networks.

Your communication plan will need to include several methods of communicating the message. Publishing articles in the employee newsletter will not suffice to win you converts to your change effort. Several different forms of media will be needed to ensure the message is moving through the organization and to reinforce the importance of the message. Look at how you can use different media to reinforce each other and the message. Your plan will want to address the use of interpersonal, audiovisual, print, and other media, such as voice and electronic mail (see Communication Media box at left).

## Group Dynamics

As you begin working with groups to bring about desired change, you will need to have an understanding of group dynamics. Individuals come into groups worried about personal identity, how well they will relate with others, and how will team membership affect their work responsibilities.

Personal identity issues include:

- Will I belong?
- Can I fit in?
- Will I be listened to?
- Will I have a chance to contribute?

Relationship issues include:

- Will everyone get along?
- How will people from different departments and levels interact?
- Will the working atmosphere be friendly or businesslike?
- Will communication be open?

Groups develop in a number of ways. A common theory of group development involves the movement of the group through five stages: forming, storming, norming, performing, and adjourning (see the box on the next page).

## COMMUNICATION MEDIA

### Interpersonal
Town meetings
Employee forums
One-on-one counseling
Orientation meetings
Brown-bag lunches

### Print
Letters
Memos
Brochures
Booklets
Pamphlets
Newsletters
Posters
Flyers

### Audiovisual
Videotapes
Teleconferences
Audio cassettes

### Other
Telephone hotlines
Voice mail
E-mail
Bulletin boards
Exhibits
"The grapevine"
Paycheck stuffers

In the forming stage, the group members are getting to know each other. During storming, the group members work on ironing out differences. Norming is the beginning of group consensus about roles and norms. Performing is when the group works together to accomplish its goals. Adjourning is when the group's work is done and the group disbands.

As the group develops, you will want to begin by looking at how the group is structured, which is determined by the roles group members take on and the norms that dictate behavior.

Roles define a function within the group. Roles may be permanent or temporary. For example, the group may elect leaders such as the president, vice president, and secretary, roles which generally last for a year or more. Roles such as team leader, recorder, or timekeeper might be assigned at each meeting in order to give everyone in the team the opportunity to learn and perform in each team role.

Roles set forth expectations in terms of how a person in a particular role is expected to act in terms of duties and in relation to others. For example, the role of president carries with it certain expectations about the duties performed and who the president consults with in the performance of those duties.

Conflict within the group can be lessened by writing down what the group roles will be and what is expected from each role. Explicit role definition gives each group member clear guidance about how the group expects each role to be filled.

While defining the roles provides guidance on what is expected from each role, norms define the behavior of the group as a whole. Norms help group members know what is expected of them in various situations. Because norms result from interaction among members, they cannot be imposed from outside. Norms might include things such as all members must take part in group discussions, members must not interrupt when another member is talking, all members will be on time for meetings, and so on. Usually, groups will reward behavior that conforms to norms and punish that which does not.

Generally, groups come together in order to accomplish goals. In order to do that, the group needs to maintain good working relationships and

# Stages of Group Development

## Forming

In this stage, group members focus on personal relationships, looking to the group leader for guidance. Group members are "sizing up" each other. Safety is a high priority for members, who desire to be accepted by the group as a whole. For this reason, serious topics are avoided at this stage. Members are orienting themselves to the group task at hand, defining the task and how to approach it.

## Storming

Conflict and competition are evident in this stage as the group members begin to hash out how they will approach their task. Listening skills are important in this stage in order for group members to move from conflict over how to approach the task to actual problem solving.

## Norming

At this stage, the group has achieved cohesiveness, has a high level of trust, and all members are actively involved in solving the task at hand. Leadership is shared, there is a great amount of creativity, and there is much sharing of data and feedback among members. Although the group is working well, concerns about the approaching breakup of the group may cause anxiety.

## Performing

This is the stage that separates high-performing teams from others, as it is a stage not often achieved by many groups. The group is interdependent, able to work as individuals, subgroups, or together. The group is focused on problem solving, yet doesn't ignore the need to attend to personal relations, leading to optimal solutions and group dynamics.

## Adjourning

The group dissolves. As the thought of ending the group can create stress, group members need a way to recognize their achievements and say their goodbyes. A planned ending, such as a celebration or other ritual, will help group members mark the end of their formal group relationship.

the ability to develop and adapt to changes in order to continue to be effective.

The keys to forming a well-functioning group include ensuring the following:

- goals are clearly stated and understood
- roles and norms are defined and adhered to
- members communicate ideas clearly
- participation and leadership are shared
- decision-making is understood and flexible
- conflict is encouraged and well managed
- power and influence are shared

As a change manager, your ability to understand the different phases of group development and the influence of roles and norms on the group will help ensure that groups are working properly and that the individual needs of group members are being met.

## Process Consultation

The change manager will use skills in process consultation to observe groups and provide feedback as a way for the group to learn how to operate more effectively. It is a skill that requires keen powers of observation, seeing how individuals and the group interact and the effects of those interactions. In response to your observations, you will provide feedback that will help the group better accomplish its task.

As a process consultant, you will be helping the group move more effectively through its development stages. Your focus will be on intervening quickly to deal with behavior that is prohibiting the group from reaching optimum performance. One caveat to remember is that while you are there to help the group improve its functioning, the process consultant is not a part of the group. Your job is to help them work better in order to solve the problem they were given; your job is not to solve the problem for them. The process consultant differs from the facilitator in that the facilitator may or may not be a member of the group, and the facilitator is usually more focused on task accomplishment.

Process consultants need an understanding of the processes occurring within the group. Process within a group refers to how the group is getting

work done, while content refers to the work the group is doing. Groups work on two processes: task and maintenance. The task process focuses on how the work is done, while maintenance process focuses on the group's social needs. It is up to the process consultant to intervene in both the task and maintenance processes.

If you relate process consultation to group development, the process consultant will be intervening more in groups in the forming, storming, and norming phases. By the time the group reaches performing, the process consultant's interventions should rarely be needed. During those first three phases of group development, the process consultant will ensure that there is balance between the focus on content, task, and maintenance, and that the group is working through each phase.

There are five types of interventions used by process consultants: Cognitive, skill and activity, behavior description, emotional/reflective, and interpretive.

■ *Cognitive Interventions*
These interventions are abstract, intellectual, or idea oriented, focusing on how the group is going to accomplish the task.

■ *Skill and Activity Interventions*
These involve the suggestion that training in a certain area will help the group achieve its goals. For example, perhaps the group can move ahead if it had better active listening skills or better understood ways to give and receive feedback.

■ *Behavior Description Interventions*
This type of intervention involves the process consultant remarking on observed behavior within the group. This would involve pointing out behaviors that are contrary to the group's agreed upon norms. For example, if the group has agreed that decision making will be done by polling for consensus, the process consultant will point out incidents when the norm is not being followed.

■ *Emotional/Reflective Interventions*
An emotional/reflective intervention would focus on observed feelings within the group. The process consultant would ask questions to surface what the reasons are behind the feelings that are being expressed.

■ *Interpretation Interventions*

These interventions often follow behavior or emotional/reflective interventions. In this intervention, the process consultant offers a proposed reason for what is seen occurring in the group in order to prompt discussion among the group members about what is happening.

Interventions may take place at the group, interpersonal, or individual level. Things to look for in determining whether or not you need to intervene include:

**Goal clarity.** Is the group clear about its goal?

**Goal direction.** Is the group working well together toward achieving the goal?

**Tone.** What tone of voice are members using with each other? Is there a need to uncover the feelings behind statements?

**Energy.** What is the group's energy level? Are they dragging, frenetic, stimulated?

**Physical posture.** What does the nonverbal language tell you?

**Tension.** Are tensions being surfaced and dealt with?

**Tracking.** Is the group staying on track overall? In discussion, are they following up on each other or changing topics?

**Task/maintenance balance.** Is there a good balance between task and maintenance processes?

**Use of humor.** Is there no humor? Is humor used destructively?

**Use of interventions by the group.** Is the group responding to the interventions? If not, why not?

Being able to give feedback is key to making interventions work. There needs to be an understanding between the process consultant and the team about how feedback will be given and received. When giving feedback, keep in mind the following:

- Know when to give feedback.
- Give both positive and negative feedback.
- Know how to give feedback.

- Be descriptive
- Don't use labels.
- Don't exaggerate.
- Don't be judgmental.

The use of interventions will help the group productively move through its development stages, increasing the likelihood that the group will indeed reach the performing phase and become a high-performing team.

## Facilitation

As previously noted, the facilitator may or may not be a member of the group itself. In some cases, the process consultant and facilitator may be one in the same. A facilitator who also serves a team as a process consultant needs to be skilled in group dynamics and process consultation as outlined above.

Facilitators generally work to help the group focus on task accomplishment. As facilitator, you need to be able to accomplish a number of things with the group, including:

- reaching consensus
- staying on task
- focusing on problem solving
- controlling flow of contributions
- rewarding and motivating members

A good facilitator does not allow one group member to dominate conversation. He or she will draw out the thoughts of quiet members. The facilitator takes ideas from the group and helps members reach consensus on how to merge those ideas. Facilitators need to be:

- good time managers who understand how to run meetings effectively

- able to focus the team on the issue at hand, bringing the group back to the topic when conversation drifts

- good listeners and accepting of others

An outside facilitator needs to remain neutral and keep quiet when the group is self-facilitating.

# Full Circle Skills and Interventions

No matter how well the analysis and intervention selection steps of the human improvement performance process have been done, good research and good solutions will not survive poor implementation. This makes the change manager's role critical to the success of the entire process. Three key abilities necessary for successful change management are:

1. Understanding the change process.

2. Building commitment to the change.

3. Providing leadership and a sense of purpose.

A number of behavioral competencies in the areas of intervention implementation, interpersonal skills, and group process management have been identified that the change manager should possess in order to help ensure successful change implementation. The intervention implementation skills enable you to:

- give management responsibility by working with their ideas

- bring management and employees together to discuss the intervention

- interview and question key people to bring them together and identify goals

- consult stakeholders before recommending changes

- adequately prepare for meetings

- model desired behavior for clients

- bring top-level management together to collaborate in the intervention

- regularly check with group members to make sure their needs are being met

- change the model and approach to help facilitate the intervention

The interpersonal skills enable you to:

- listen to clients and work with their ideas

- use questions effectively

- listen to all issues and not downgrade any

- use listening and paraphrasing skills to understand the client's perspective

The group process management skills:

- allow the group to identify areas they would like to work on

- patiently let the group find its own answers to problems

- discuss problems to help manage conflict

- keep the group focused on positive aspects of the intervention

- do not allow the group to be overly critical of a single member's ideas

- acknowledge all the concerns of the group and deal with each one

- listen to all issues, while staying with the overall issue

- summarize the feelings of an individual that are impeding progress of the group

- defuse heated issues

- speak privately to an individual about a particular problem so as not to interfere with group process

Generally, the best change consultants are open and responsive to others, are comfortable with ambiguity and able to make sense of it, and are comfortable with themselves in relation to others.

While there is no "one right way" to bring about change, the more of these identified skills and behaviors the change manager possesses the more likely the success of the implementation process. For those interested in helping manage the change process, acquiring these skills and behaviors through training or experience is a step in the right direction.

# References & Resources

## Articles

Barron, Tom. "The Road Toward Performance: Three Vignettes." *Technical & Skills Training,* January 1997, pp. 12-14.

Burns, Greg. "The Secrets of Team Facilitation." *Training & Development,* June 1995, pp. 46-52.

Church, Allan H., et al. "OD Practitioners as Facilitator of Change: An Analysis of Survey Results." *Group & Organization Management,* March 1996, pp. 22-66.

Donovan, Michael and Leta Letize. "Lessons from the Wizard." *Journal for Quality and Participation,* July/August 1993, pp. 44-47.

Hunn, Michael S. and Steven I. Meisel. "Internal Communication: Auditing for Quality." *Quality Progress,* June 1991, pp. 56-60.

Knapp, Richard J. "Six and a Half Steps for Effective Communication." *Topics in Total Compensation,* Vol. 3, No. 4, pp. 319-325.

Krackhardt, David and Jeffrey R. Hanson, "Informal Networks: The Company Behind the Chart." *Harvard Business Review,* July/August 1993, pp. 104-111.

Lauer, Larry D. "How to Improve Internal Communication: Guidelines for the Nonprofit Manager." *Nonprofit World,* Vol. 12, No. 3, pp. 34-38.

Lawrie, John. "The ABCs of Change Management." *Training & Development Journal,* March 1990, pp. 87-89.

Longman-Czeropski, Susan. "Follow the Leader." *Quality Progress,* December 1994, pp. 47-49.

O'Driscoll, Michael and James L. Eubanks. "Behavioral Competencies, Goal Setting, and OD Practitioner Effectiveness" *Group & Organization Management,* September 1993, pp. 308-327.

Schein, Edgar. "A General Philosophy of Helping: Process Consultation." *Sloan Management Review,* Spring 1990, pp. 57-64.

## Books

ASTD. *Introduction to Performance: A Primer for Trainers.* Alexandria, Virginia: American Society for Training & Development, 1996.

Brown, Mark Grahan, et al. *Rx For Business: A Troubleshooting Guide for Building a High Performance Organization.* Chicago, Illinois: Irwin Professional Publishing, 1996.

Connor, Patrick E. and Linda K. Lake. *Managing Organizational Change.* 2nd ed. Westport, Connecticut: Praeger, 1994.

Craig, Robert L., (ed). *The ASTD Training and Development Handbook: A Guide to Human Resource Development.* 4th ed. New York: McGraw-Hill, 1996.

Egan, Gerard. *Change-Agent Skills B: Managing Innovation and Change.* San Diego, California: University Associates, Inc., 1988.

Johnson, David W. and Frank P. Johnson. *Joining Together: Group Theory and Group Skills.* 5th ed. Boston, Massachusetts: Allyn and Bacon, 1994.

# References & Resources

Kirkpatrick, Donald L. *How to Manage Change Effectively.* San Francisco: Jossey-Bass, 1985.

Odiorne, George S. *The Change Resisters: How They Prevent Progress and What Managers Can Do about Them.* Englewood Cliffs, New Jersey: Prentice-Hall, 1981.

Reddy, W. Brendan. *Intervention Skills: Process Consultation for Small Groups and Teams.* Amsterdam, The Netherlands: Pfeiffer & Company, 1994.

Robinson, Dana G. and James C. Robinson. *Performance Consulting: Moving Beyond Training.* San Francisco: Berrett-Koehler, 1995.

Rothwell, William J. *ASTD Models for Human Performance Improvement: Roles, Competencies, and Outputs.* Alexandria, Virginia: American Society for Training & Development, 1996.

Rummler, Geary A. and Alan P. Brache. *Improving Performance: Managing the White Space on the Organization Chart.* San Francisco: Jossey-Bass, 1996.

Scholtes, Peter R. *The Team Handbook: How to Use Teams to Improve Quality.* Madison, Wisconsin: Joiner Associates, 1988.

Stolovitch, Harold D. and Erica J. Keeps, (eds.). *Handbook of Human Performance Technology: A Comprehensive Guide for Analyzing and Solving Performance Problems in Organizations.* San Francisco: Jossey-Bass, 1992.

Swanson, Richard A. *Analysis for Improving Performance: Tools for Diagnosing Organizations and Documenting Workplace Expertise.* San Francisco: Berrett-Koehler, 1996.

*The Best of Organizational Change.* Alexandria, Virginia: American Society for Training & Development, 1992.

Tichy, Noel M. and Mary Anne Devanna. *The Transformational Leader.* New York: John Wiley and Sons, 1990.

## Info-lines

Callahan, Madelyn R. "From Training to Performance Consulting." No. 9702.

———. "The Role of the Performance Evaluator." No. 9803.

———. "The Role of the Performance Intervention Specialist." No. 9714.

Carr, Don A. "How to Facilitate," No. 9406.

Gill, S.J. "Linking Training to Performance Goals." No. 9606.

Kirrane, Diane. "The Role of the Performance Needs Analyst." No. 9713.

# The Role of the
# Performance Evaluator

Issue 9803

# The Role of the Performance Evaluator

**AUTHOR:**

Madelyn Callahan

**Editor**
Cat Sharpe

**Designer**
Steven M. Blackwood

**Copy Editor**
Kay Larson

**ASTD Internal Consultant**
Phil Anderson

# The Performance Evaluator

The human performance improvement (HPI) process consists of identifying performance gaps, researching interventions to close performance gaps, selecting the right interventions for the particular problems, and assessing the degree to which the selected interventions helped close the performance gaps. The last phase of the process, assessment of the selected interventions, describes the HPI evaluator's key responsibility—measuring and evaluating the impact of the intervention on specific performance gaps or organizational goals.

Much like all evaluation processes, HPI evaluation is ongoing throughout the performance improvement process. The evaluator may assist the analyst during the initial phase of the process in identifying the gap between real and desired performance levels.

As the HPI process continues, so do evaluation efforts. The evaluator is on hand to provide continuous feedback that may effect further changes, to help organizations develop continuous tracking systems to ensure that organizational goals are being addressed and fulfilled, and to assist in the creation of pilot or small-scale efforts that cause minimal disruption to business operations but generate meaningful evaluation data.

At the end of the process, once the intervention has been completed, the evaluator measures or helps others to measure the effectiveness of the intervention by again assessing the difference between actual and ideal performance.

In short, the HPI evaluator takes an active role throughout the improvement process. He or she takes part in identifying and diagnosing problems, assessing the effectiveness of interventions, and clarifying organizational and performance goals and objectives. This issue of *Info-line* will give you a detailed look at the role of the evaluator in the HPI process by describing what the evaluator does, the skills and competencies required to do the job, and how the evaluator's work enhances the value of the HPI process.

# Role of the Evaluator

The primary job of the evaluator is *to assess the impact and results* of the intervention. He or she must examine all changes, actions taken to effect change, and the outcomes of these efforts. The evaluator must then report his or her findings on how interventions are being implemented to stakeholders and participants.

In evaluating the intervention outcome, the evaluator examines the target of the change effort—for example, productivity-based employee performance—and the means or intervention used to effect the change—such as an incentive program. The evaluator measures outcomes to determine the amount of change and improvement that has resulted.

The evaluator must determine the degree to which:

- the intervention accomplished predetermined, quantifiable results

- the results matched the intended effect of the interventions

- the gap between desired and actual performance has closed

- organizational needs were fulfilled

- the corporate culture adopted the intervention

Evaluation should also reveal the positive and negative effects of the intervention, details about apparent side effects, and corrective guidance for future intervention efforts.

## Competency and Skill Requirements

The evaluator must have specific skills and competencies to be able to properly assess the rate of progress and the effect of an intervention. He or she must be skilled and competent in the following areas:

1. Measuring performance gaps.

2. Evaluating results against organizational goals.

3. Establishing standards.

4. Assessing organizational culture effects.

**5.** Reviewing interventions.

**6.** Providing feedback.

To carry out assessments, evaluators must be able to perform actions and produce outcomes related to each skill. Following are examples for each area of competency.

**Measuring performance gaps.** To measure the performance gap, evaluators must:

- Set objectives for the HPI evaluation.

- Put together plans and designs for the HPI evaluation.

- Create or select evaluation instruments.

- Establish standards for measuring performance.

- Measure performance before and after the intervention.

- Produce recommendations, conclusions, and findings.

- Prepare reports on the HPI results for managers and employees.

**Evaluating results against organizational goals.** In assessing how well the results of interventions match organizational goals, evaluators must:

- link the intervention to other change efforts in the organization

- ensure individual interventions share common goals

- create a link between the intervention and the organization's plans, goals, and objectives

- focus the intent of the intervention on supporting and improving the organization's business needs

**Establishing standards.** To successfully set standards, evaluators must establish performance standards and communicate the performance standards.

**Assessing organizational culture effects.** To measure the impact on the organizational culture, evaluators must link the intervention to the organization's culture.

**Reviewing interventions.** To find ways to continuously improve an intervention before and during implementation, evaluators must provide written and oral reports to stakeholders and participants about the progress of the intervention.

**Providing feedback.** When supplying feedback, evaluators must collect and provide information about:

- the progress of the intervention to the organization, to the affected teams or work groups, and to management

- performance to the organization, to the affected teams or work groups, and to management

## The Evaluation Process

It has been noted in *The Handbook of Human Performance Technology* that "Evaluation always appears last on any list of process steps…but it is important to note that, for the HPI specialist, evaluation starts in step 1—the problem or opportunity identification, where the performance to be improved is identified."

With this in mind, evaluations may be conducted according to four different categories of criteria.

### ■ *Behavior*
The key word here is performance—as it relates specifically to on-the-job behavior that should have been affected by the HPI intervention. The evaluator will want to know, for example, if the performer is using new skills and knowledge on the job, or if a change in job design, workflow, operations, job aids, or some other intervention has influenced any improvement in performance.

The evaluator must collect performance data before the intervention so that he or she can compare that data to post-intervention performance data. In this way the evaluator may determine whether the intervention has had an impact on performance.

### ■ *Reaction*
It is important to know how the performers, who are the focus of the intervention, felt about it.

Evaluators will want to know if they were satisfied with the intervention, and the degree to which they found it useful and relevant. If they didn't like it, evaluators will ask for specific reasons why the intervention was unsatisfactory.

The objective is to size up performers' opinions of intervention activity content, the amount of time it took, and the overall quality of the effort. It's important to note performers' attitudes going into the intervention process—were they positive and open to it, or reluctant and turned off?

■ *Learning*
If the intervention involved intended changes in skills, knowledge, or attitudes, the evaluator will want to assess the extent to which the performers changed—how much of the intervention content they took in and comprehended, how much knowledge and how many new skills they acquired.

This type of assessment takes place directly after the intervention and focuses solely on the degree of learning as separate from learning that's transferred to the job. To accurately measure the effectiveness of the intervention, pre- and post-intervention assessments should be conducted.

■ *Results*
When evaluators measure results, they are trying to determine whether the intervention produced the desired impact on the organization—that is, whether the intervention helped accomplish some of the organization's goals. For example, if the intervention was used to focus on improving sales, the evaluator will examine the effect the intervention had on the organization's sales goals for the quarter.

## Approaches to Evaluation

Some evaluators divide the ways to measure variables into two broad categories. According to this way of thinking, measures that are based on judgment or opinion are considered subjective evaluation observations of events; actions or other variables that are clear and require little if any judgment are considered objective evaluations.

The evaluator has an active part in phases throughout the HPI process. Here are some examples of when to perform evaluations:

# Dealing with Obstacles

In every work environment, HPI evaluators can expect to encounter some obstacles to implementing the evaluation process. Here are some examples of common problems and tips for addressing them:

■ *Limited Time*
Staff should know that though they feel they may not have time to perform a comprehensive evaluation, such efforts actually save time later. Once the staff learns how an intervention must be adjusted, reworked, or actually cut in its entirety, they'll be able to see why the work of a thorough evaluation program is critical. The more they plan and work on the process at the front end, the more time they'll save during the follow-up phase for the general evaluation.

■ *Too Complex a Process*
If the work looks too difficult to put into practice, have staff reduce each large step to smaller, more manageable tasks. Breaking out components will simplify and make the overall process less threatening.

■ *Lack of Motivation*
Though senior management may not require the evaluation, staff must still be motivated to perform it. Staff members should be helped to understand the benefits of performing a thorough evaluation, even if management does not encourage or push accountability.

■ *Fear of Criticism*
Staff reluctance may also reflect their fear of criticism. Many people feel that evaluations will reveal results that will be used to criticize individuals. Try to reassure people that the information you collect will be applied only toward improving the intervention project.

### Before an Intervention

During the performance analysis and cause analysis phase, evaluation is used to:

• identify problems

• develop objectives for the intervention

• select interventions

• determine the best ways to actually evaluate the interventions

### During Intervention Development

During the intervention selection and design phases, evaluation is used to decide whether:

- a proposed intervention may be useful or relevant to the target population

- the intervention's design is appropriate and perhaps select other design options

- the intervention itself meets the design specifications of the development team

### Following the Intervention

During and after implementation, evaluation is used to:

- assess the impact on the target audience

- determine whether the intervention has had an effect on performance

- measure whether the performance gap has begun to close

- note changes in performers' attitudes by observing their reactions to the intervention

- determine any effect on organizational goals

## Measuring Performance Gaps

The job of measuring or helping others to measure the impact of an intervention by assessing the difference between actual and ideal performance is the key to the role of the evaluator. Following are some basic steps involved in ascertaining that difference:

1. Establish the definition of ideal performance. To find out what desired performance includes, you need information about the organization's expectations for the particular job performance.

2. Establish the definition of real or current performance. To determine the level of performance for most employees, you need information about how the organization perceives the quality of work by a majority of the workforce.

3. Compare organizational performance standards with current performance data.

In the steps above, the performance gap is the difference between ideal and actual performance. Productivity rates, product quality, and cost-benefit ratios are just a few of the ways the evaluator can measure actual performance. Here are some additional facts about these standards of measurement:

■ *Productivity Rates*
Performance may be directly linked to the number of products manufactured in a set period of time; this measurement may apply to organizational, divisional, and individual objectives for performance.

■ *Product Quality*
Another measurement with applications to performance at all levels of the organization, quality assessment takes into account errors and the numbers of products that do not meet quality standards and therefore cannot be delivered.

■ *Costs and Benefits*
At the point of measuring a performance gap, a cost-benefit analysis would examine the current costs associated with sub-par performance (costs of rejected products, waste, injuries, and so forth) and performance improvement needs compared with the expected gains that improved performance would deliver.

## Evaluating Results Against Intentions

Although it is important to assess the intervention's impact on performance, it is also critical to measure how well the intervention's results meet organizational goals. By this standard of measurement, the intervention will have a positive impact if it succeeds in helping the organization achieve its goals. Here are some tips and considerations for making this comparison:

**Link specific intervention outcomes** to corresponding business needs and strategic goals. For example, improvements in customer service techniques may be directly connected to a significant rise in sales and decline in customer complaints.

**Give the intervention time.** Organizational goals and objectives are often based on the big picture, indicating a focus on longer-term effects and larger-scale achievements. To be able to study the impact and get an accurate measurement of true results, you must allow an adequate length of time to pass.

**Review the group's goals for productivity,** quality improvement, quality of work life, communication and human relations, reduced costs, leadership and time management, increased sales, or other areas. Compare pre-intervention figures for these areas with post-intervention numbers and note any differences that may be the result of your change efforts.

**Practice "mapping" organizational goals** to individual performance goals. Mapping is an approach that traces the impact of each performance intervention to overall business objectives.

For example, begin with an organizational goal such as a 10 percent drop in production costs. Trace that to a departmental goal of reduced costs, stemming from an intervention to change a business process. Link the attainment of the departmental goal to individual performance goals.

Mapping not only identifies causal links between business and individual performance goals, it also reveals cases where links are not in place, and HPI interventions have failed to produce performance that contributes to achieving business goals.

Note whether the performance improvement is continual. The achievement of organizational goals requires ongoing improvement efforts. As you evaluate intervention results against organizational goals, look at ways the performance improvement may have added value to the organization's products and services. In addition to telling managers about the intervention's success, it's important to also show them how outcomes link directly to business goals. This kind of communication helps managers become involved in the performance improvement process. They can provide support and assistance in developing and reinforcing interventions and helping ensure long-term relevance for change efforts.

## Measuring Outcomes and Impact

Evaluation may apply to the outcome of a performance or process, or to a product. For example, the job of a safety compliance team or the compliance process may be evaluated on the basis of how many injuries have taken place in the unit and whether safety compliance audits are being conducted on a regular basis. A safety manual may be assessed to determine its effectiveness for guiding safety personnel in using the correct procedures.

For the most part, outcomes refer to the results of an intervention directly after it has taken place. Impact may refer to the intervention's effect over time and beyond the workplace. For example, the impact of a good safety policy and program would be evident in the public's perception of the company, in the way clients feel about doing business with the company, and ultimately in the rate of profits or return on stockholders' investments.

Here are some considerations when undertaking evaluations of outcomes and impacts:

- Distinguish between the evaluations of shorter-term, localized outcomes and those for more wide-ranging, longer-term impacts.

- Do both because each yields valuable data the organization needs for planning future efforts.

- Take your place among the initiators in the process; you'll be glad later that you did. That is, evaluators have a role in the analysis phase. You know that your early evaluations of needs and problems will be essential to later evaluation of intervention results.

- As much and as often as you can, bring in financial indicators and similar issues that have key significance to top management. Bottom-line considerations have enormous significance in all aspects of business planning, but they are particularly relevant in determining the funding and future of all intervention efforts.

- Tie findings to overall business and organizational goals.

- Evaluate more than one variable.

- Evaluate often and thoroughly.

# Evaluation: A Model

Keep in mind that evaluation is not a one-stop, final effort at tabulating results. It is part of the HPI process from the initial planning and analysis to the final ROI calculations. At all points throughout the intervention there will always be opportunities to evaluate and provide feedback as you assist in fine-tuning a pilot effort or help with final revisions in preparation for launching the intervention. To get an idea where evaluation may take place along the way, look at these selected points in the HPI process:

### ■ *Perform Gap Analysis and Draft Objectives*
This step may be prompted by deficient performance, productivity problems, management call for training, need to meet a government requirement, or attempts to boost employee morale. Baseline data reflects the problem with performance. It should be collected over a significant period of time so that meaningful before-and-after comparisons can be made.

### ■ *State Evaluation's Purpose*
Identify the reasons for the evaluation so you can plan or design methods and instruments appropriately. The reasons will also affect the baseline data you will be collecting. An evaluation may be needed to measure the intervention's contribution to performance improvement; decide the future of the intervention, whether to continue, expand, or terminate the program; or upgrade the resources used in the intervention program.

### ■ *Select Approaches, Methods, and Design*
In deciding how to evaluate, consider such important factors as the work environment, the performers who will be directly affected by the evaluation, and the content of the intervention. Examples of methods include before-and-after performance measurements; feedback from performers and their supervisors, customers, and upper management; interviews with all stakeholders; performance appraisals and contracts; and observation of performers on the job or in job simulations.

### ■ *Decide on a Strategy*
This will help determine how to evaluate the intervention. One individual should be designated to gather and analyze the evaluation data and then report it to all stakeholders. When the evaluation should take place is a question that depends on careful planning. It may be necessary to establish several different dates for collecting initial and follow-up data to ensure that all important questions are answered.

### ■ *Determine Intervention Program Objectives*
Make sure they are measurable and linked to needs as assessed. Each objective should relate specifically to the collected baseline data.

### ■ *Calculate Expected Return-on-Investment*
First find out what the intervention's estimated costs and benefits will be. Establish estimates of costs to develop and conduct the intervention and compare them with the anticipated benefits of the intervention. If the need for the intervention surpasses all economic considerations, you may decide to forgo establishing estimates. Your focus may then be on maintaining reasonable costs and maximum efficiency in the development and delivery of the intervention program.

## Establishing Standards

Too often people confuse standards with objectives. Most organizations know what they want their people to achieve because the organization has established business goals. But few explain to people how they must behave or perform in order to achieve their individual goals that are linked to the organization's goals.

To find out what behaviors are correct and will lead to accomplishing goals, performers must have standards. They need specific performance requirements for ideal performance. In addition,

they need to know that the organization expects them to fulfill these requirements. Following are some facts about standards:

● Standards describe preferred performance for achieving organizational goals.

● They may apply to individuals, processes, or organizations.

● Examples of performance standards for individuals include sales made, widgets produced, errors made, calls answered, and customers served.

■ *Present Plans to Top Management*

To garner management support and gain acceptance, provide estimates and evaluation plans in a formal presentation and proposal.

■ *Create and Build Evaluation Instruments*

You may also choose to select existing instruments. These tools are used to gather data on the intervention's results and performance changes. Examples of tools include questionnaires, tests, surveys, interviews, focus groups, and observations. The best tools are easy to apply and reliable in terms of accuracy.

■ *Test Intervention and Revise Problem Areas*

A trial run of the intervention program may be most valuable for interventions that will be repeated with large groups. During this portion of the planning process, evaluators have an opportunity to test and adjust some of their assessment methods such as pre- and post-intervention evaluations, participants' reactions, and performance or behavior simulations. To ensure good results with your test, carefully select the pilot audience, set rules during the test, develop and encourage group unity, and flag any problems you observe.

■ *Compile Data for Further Revisions*

Devise and implement a system of collecting data at the right times throughout the process. Establish a collection schedule and follow it closely. The most elaborate and thorough evaluation plans may fail because proper data collection did not take place during the designated intervals. Be especially careful to abide by the schedule during the follow-up portion of the evaluation.

■ *Examine the Information*

Look at all the data, analyze, and interpret them. Tabulate responses on questionnaires, look at variances in before-and-after performance appraisals, compare productivity rates in audits, and so forth. Evaluate data collected during the program and make adjustments to the intervention as you go. Combine on-the-job performance data and follow-up data with other information to complete your evaluation of the entire intervention process.

■ *Adjust as Needed*

Use the data analysis to make needed changes to the intervention—or to terminate it if the data indicate that would be best. Look at those portions of the intervention program that need to be made more effective, according to the evaluation. Look into each aspect of the program to find out why it may have produced inadequate results.

■ *Calculate the Actual Return-on-Investment*

Do this calculation if you require economic justification for the intervention. The basic approach is to divide the dollar value of results by the program costs. Compare the return-on-investment to a predetermined target rate based on the organization's investment and expenditure standards or on management expectations of the intervention.

■ *Prepare Research and Results for Stakeholders*

Communicate results in an unbiased, effective way to HPI staff, who will need the data to fine-tune the intervention program in order to improve it; management and other decision makers involved with determining the future of the program; participants who need feedback on their performance in order to enhance and improve it.

---

- Examples of standards for processes may include specific levels of production quality and quantity, and length of production time.

- Performance standards for organizations may include profit levels, revenues, cost-benefit comparisons, investments, expansion of product line, sales, expansion of customer base and market share, cost cutting, and acquisitions.

To set standards, follow these guidelines:

**Talk to stakeholders** to find out what their expectations are of the performance. Interview top management, line managers, employees, clients, and others who have definite opinions about what performance level is required.

**Look at current and revised job descriptions,** formal statements about changing job expectations, and all projection studies or reports on future plans for redesigning job or division responsibilities.

**Examine organizational goals** and projected goals for the future.

**Talk to management** about any foreseeable changes to the organization that would affect performance goals and expectations—such as the purchase of a new product line or new technology, upgrading of manufacturing processes, implementation of new productivity rates or production quality standards.

## Defining Preferred Performance

The critical standard for HPI evaluation is preferred performance, which answers the question, "What does an exemplary performer do?" It is essential to any evaluation effort to have a detailed model of what the organization considers to be the ideal. To create this model you must have information pertaining to:

**Performance outcomes.** What must the performer achieve on the job, and how are these achievements linked to the organization's goals? What is the desired end product of the performer's action? These are key questions for establishing this standard.

**Competencies.** To produce these outcomes, what competencies must the performer possess? Note the behaviors of top performers. What attributes and skills do they have? What knowledge do they have that may give them an advantage? The best way to get this information is to observe and talk to the best performers. Watch what they do, and ask them how they do it. Find out what they think they must know and do to achieve their goals.

Examples of preferred performances by a compliance evaluator for a large manufacturer of chemicals may include the following:

- conducts ongoing research into the status of legislative and regulatory actions that may affect compliance duties

- obtains reliable, official direction and guidance on compliance requirements once regulations and applicable laws have taken effect

- provides communication, instruction, guidance, and training to all employees affected by compliance requirements

- conducts periodic checks on operations to determine compliance status and provides feedback as needed

- reinforces message that compliance is required by law and violations may result in serious charges and costly fines

These preferred performance behaviors may be described as the following competencies: research skills; compliance knowledge; communication skills; knowledge of the legislative and regulatory processes; knowledge of organizational operations affected by compliance requirements; training skills; ability to judge compliance status; and feedback skills.

■ *Criteria*
Evaluators must select or develop a context or basis, specific to the type of job, for gauging the quality of the performance outcome. For example, measurements for the job of compliance evaluator might include:

- no warnings or citations by federal, state, or local agencies charged with monitoring the organization's operations

- full compliance with all applicable regulations; active participation by line managers and employees in discussions of how to comply with regulations in a thorough and timely manner

- accomplishment of goals related to eliminating the incidence of injuries and costly mistakes on the job

■ *Environment*
What influences inside and outside the organization are pushing the achievement of the best performance or creating obstacles to it? Examples of positive factors affecting product may include:

- periodic check-ups that select a random sampling of products for review; quality team meetings that promote and reiterate the benefits of maintaining quality products for all members of the organization

- spot training offered to help individuals and groups fine-tune production skills

Factors that may detract from achieving quality standards may include the following: too-high

## How-to's for Mapping

To "map" performance results at the different levels throughout the organization, try to keep each process separate and focused and the various elements in order. The table below may help you simplify things.

| To Measure: | Use These Methods: |
|---|---|
| Overall performance goals for an organization | • interviews with executives<br>• quarterly and annual reports<br>• business status reports |
| Performance goals of individual departments and units | • customer satisfaction surveys<br>• progress reports from line managers<br>• interviews with senior managers within the department |
| Improvement in operations and processes | • customer satisfaction surveys<br>• senior management reports<br>• progress reports from line managers<br>• interviews with managers and customers<br>• observations |
| Employee output objectives | • production reports<br>• observations<br>• monitoring data<br>• job analysis data |
| Job behaviors after the intervention | • employee job assessments<br>• observations<br>• self-assessment tools<br>• skills and performance tests<br>• performance appraisals |
| Future performance improvement needs of employees | • comparison of performance to earlier levels<br>• observations<br>• tests<br>• surveys<br>• questionnaires<br>• interviews |

rates of production that may force performers or units to try to cut corners to meet their quotas by deadline, or improper or inadequate maintenance on equipment; lack of communication or cooperation between divisions that must work together to achieve success.

### Information Sources

Examples of sources to use in setting standards, evaluating intervention results or pre-intervention status, and assessing the organization-wide effect of interventions include any of the following:

• interviews
• files
• documents
• observations
• feedback, both formal and informal
• annual reports and quarterly reports
• managers' and supervisors' reports
• job monitoring data
• production reports
• customer satisfaction surveys
• business status reports

- quality levels
- operations reviews
- questionnaires or "smile sheets"
- before-and-after intervention knowledge tests
- exit interviews and other follow-up services

## Measuring Impact on Culture

How do a performance gap and an HPI intervention affect the organizational culture—that is, what is the impact on commonly held beliefs about correct or incorrect workplace behaviors? To measure this, use the following checklist of points:

☐ Assess the effect on beliefs by measuring any changes in attitude.

☐ Find out what values and beliefs were commonly held before the intervention; compare them to post-intervention beliefs and values.

☐ Talk to people to find out what they think. Ask performers in interviews and on satisfaction surveys about their perceptions.

☐ Observe people. Take note of whether there are changes in behaviors that may be related to the intervention and to cultural factors.

☐ Note whether people seem motivated to use the intervention that is targeted to change the organizational culture.

☐ Talk to managers about what they've observed in the workplace and what they may be experiencing as the intervention's effect on the culture.

☐ Talk to the designers and developers of the intervention and find out how they intended the intervention to affect organizational culture. Ask them if they feel the intervention has made an impact.

## Reviewing Interventions

A key responsibility for the evaluator is to assess HPI interventions during both the design and implementation phases. Consistent monitoring and evaluation provide an effective strategy for keeping the process on course and linked to the objectives set at the beginning of the effort.

During these points, your success in making meaningful contributions and voicing any concerns or recommendations to the right sources may depend on a variety of factors. Here are some observations and ideas for ensuring success.

**Measure the change effort** with a clear focus on and for the dedicated purpose of continuing improvement throughout the intervention process.

**Measure process along with results.** The more fine-tuning and adjustment to the intervention process, the more valuable the results will be. Before and during the intervention, evaluators will

## Who Are Key Stakeholders?

Anyone who has a stake in the intervention process will be affected by the evaluation phase. It is important to remember that a majority of stakeholders may be key players in organizational matters and that addressing their needs may be important to garnering support for future HPI efforts.

Including as many stakeholders as possible in the evaluation process or in your communications about the process will be advantageous. Satisfying stakeholders may bring about needed cooperation from various sources, assistance in selecting the proper context for the evaluation report, and help in producing a balanced, realistic interpretation of evaluation results. Stakeholders may provide assistance in developing the evaluation process, establishing points of focus and appropriate standards, suggesting the types of data that should be compiled, and recommending approaches or methods for collecting information.

Stakeholders may include:

**Front-line managers** who need information to use in tracking day-to-day operations.

**Top management** who focus on conclusions and bottom-line data that will help them decide whether to continue, broaden, or terminate an intervention effort.

**Intervention designers** who should be encouraged to participate early in the evaluation effort.

**Participants in the interventions** who are employees and others directly involved in change efforts focusing on training, operations, productivity goals, or performance incentive programs.

**Managers or supervisors of those participants** who have a stake in the overall performance of their units or divisions.

have opportunities to go over intervention requirements, emphases, activities, and other factors that significantly influence results.

**Keep participants' needs** in mind during reviews. Evaluators may examine whether all aspects of the intervention are appropriate for the target audience and their needs, whether modifications to the original design affect the intervention's established objectives and direction, and whether management's expectations for performance should change with adjustments to the process.

**Use the information to make timely** and relevant changes to the process. As you learn more about the organization's goals, you can better understand that the process of continuing improvement affects all levels of the organization. As you regularly assess people's progress during the intervention you may find the organization motivated to reassess and clarify its goals.

**Focus on using assessment to improve,** not to lay blame. Let participants know that the objective is to improve performance, and to do so by first improving the intervention process. If performers feel threatened or singled out as an example of poor performance, they will be reluctant to cooperate with any change efforts.

**Follow through on your promise.** Once you've told participants how the data will be used, follow through; show them that you are using the evaluation data for the sole purpose of improving intervention activities and other changes that will contribute to better performance.

## Providing Feedback

Feedback is a part or aspect of the evaluation phase. It focuses on providing incremental information to improve the process that results in a performance or product. People sometimes confuse it with evaluation, which is the action taken to assess or assign value to performance, processes, or products. For more detailed information on feedback, refer to *Info-line* No. 9006, "Coaching and Feedback."

Essentially, evaluation appears most like feedback when it is applied to point out problem areas and indicate improvements. Feedback on job performance may be provided in a variety of ways, either formally or informally. The purpose of a feedback system is to link real or actual performance to specific standards of preferred or ideal performance. In every system, clear and straightforward communication is the key to guiding performance. Following are facts about feedback and suggestions for presenting it:

- Feedback is most commonly used to correct job performance behaviors or improve other performance-related issues.

- It is not generally regarded by management as a large-scale, organized effort to evaluate work products or work progress.

- For the most part, managers provide feedback only after a sub-par performance rather than an ideal one.

- It is most effective when used with clearly stated standards.

- Feedback should reinforce the correct performance behaviors.

- Feedback must be based on careful, thoughtful evaluation of the performance and the results of that performance.

- Feedback should provide guidance for changing the performance to make it acceptable.

- New performers should receive feedback directly after they have performed successfully to reinforce those positive behaviors.

A big advantage of developing an internal feedback system is that once in place, it can be used continuously. These systems provide ongoing reinforcement and guidance, which are particularly vital to curricula of new performers and those who have recently been trained to use the latest technology.

# References & Resources

## Articles

Carr, C., and L. Totzke. "The Long and Winding Path (From Instructional Technology to Performance Technology)." *Performance & Instruction*, August 1995, pp. 4-8.

Clark, R.C. "Hang Up Your Training Hat." *Training & Development*, September 1994, pp. 61-65.

Elliot, P. "Power-Charging People's Performance." *Training & Development*, December 1996, pp. 46-49.

Gephart, M.A. "The Road to High Performance." *Training & Development*, June 1995, pp. 30-38.

Middlebrook, J.F. "How To Manage Individual Performance." *Training & Development*, September 1996, pp. 45-48.

Rummler, G. "In Search of the Holy Performance Grail." *Training & Development*, April 1996, pp. 26-32.

Smalley, K., et al. "Strategic Planning: From Training to Performance Technology Within Three Years." *Performance Improvement Quarterly*, vol. 8, no. 2 (1995), pp. 114-124.

Sorohan, E.G. "The Performance Consultant at Work." *Training & Development*, March 1996, pp. 35-38.

Thiagarajan, S. "Formative Evaluation in Performance Technology." *Performance Improvement Quarterly*, vol. 4, no. 2, pp. 23-34.

———. "What to Avoid When Shifting From Training to Performance Consulting." *Training Director's Forum Newsletter*, March 1996, pp. 1-3.

## Books

ASTD. *Introduction to Performance: A Primer for Trainers*. Alexandria, Virginia: American Society for Training & Development, 1996.

———. *The Best of the Evaluation of Training*. Alexandria, Virginia: American Society for Training & Development, 1991.

Barger, N., and L. Kirby. *The Challenge of Change in Organizations: Helping Employees Thrive in the New Frontier*. North Carolina: Davies-Black Publishing, 1995.

Basarab, D.J., and D.K. Root. *The Training Evaluation Process: A Practical Approach to Evaluating Corporate Training Programs*. Norwell, Massachusetts: Kluwer Academic, 1992.

Bassi, L.J., et al. *The ASTD Training Data Book*. Alexandria, Virginia: American Society for Training & Development, 1996.

Bennis, W., and B. Nanus. *Leaders: The Strategies for Taking Charge*. New York: Harper & Row, 1985.

Block, P. *Flawless Consulting: A Guide to Getting Your Expertise Used*. San Diego, California: University Associates, 1981.

Brinkerhoff, R.O., and S.J. Gill. *The Learning Alliance*. San Francisco: Jossey-Bass, 1994.

Craig, R.L. *The ASTD Training & Development Handbook: A Guide to Human Resource Development*. (4th edition). Alexandria, Virginia: American Society for Training & Development, 1996.

Dubois, D.D. *Competency-B... mance Improvement*. Amh... chusetts: HRD Press, 199...

Gilbert, T.F. *Human Compet... neering Worthy Performar... York: McGraw-Hill, 1978.

Golembiewski, R. *Handbook ... tional Consultation*. New ... Dekker, 1993.

Gouilart, F., and J. Kelly. *Tr... the Organization: Refram... rate Direction, Restructur... pany, Revitalizing the Ent... Renewing People*. New Yo... Hill, 1995.

Graduous, D. *Systems Theor... Human Resource Develop... Alexandria, Virginia: Ame... for Training & Developm...

Holcomb, J. *Make Training ... Penny: On-Target Evalua... Diego, California: Pfeiffer...

Holtz, H. *How to Succeed as ... dent Consultant*. (3rd edit... York: Wiley, 1993.

Kaufman, R. *Strategic Planni... nizational Guide* (revised ... Newbury Park, California ... cations, 1992.

Kaufman, R., et al. *The Pract... Handbook on Organizatio... Human Performance Imp... San Diego, California: Un... ciates/Pfeiffer, 1995.

# References & Resources

## *Info-line*s

Kirkpatrick, D.L. *Evaluating Training Programs: The Four Levels.* San Francisco: Berrett-Koehler, 1994.

Mager, R.F. *Measuring Instructional Results.* (2nd edition). Belmont, California: David S. Lake Publishers, 1984.

Medsker, K.L., and D.G. Roberts. *ASTD Trainer's Toolkit: Evaluating the Results of Training.* Alexandria, Virginia: American Society for Training & Development, 1992.

Michalko, M. *Thinkertoys: A Handbook of Business Creativity for the '90s.* Berkeley, California: Ten Speed Press, 1991.

Pfeffer, J. *Power in Organizations.* Marshfield, Massachusetts: Pittman Publishing, 1981.

Phillips, J. *Handbook of Training Evaluation and Measurement Methods.* (2nd edition). Houston, Texas: Gulf Publishing, 1991.

Robinson, D.G., and J.C. Robinson. *Training for Impact: How to Link Training to Business Needs and Measure the Results.* San Francisco: Jossey-Bass, 1989.

Rothwell, W. *ASTD Models for Human Performance Improvement.* Alexandria, Virginia: American Society for Training & Development, 1996.

———. *Beyond Training and Development: State-of-the-Art Strategies for Enhancing Human Performance.* New York: AMACOM, 1996.

Rothwell, W., and H. Kazanas. *Human Resource Development: A Strategic Approach* (revised edition). Amherst, Massachusetts: HRD Press, 1994.

Rothwell, W., et al. *Practicing Organization Development: A Guide for Consultants.* San Diego, California: Pfeiffer, 1995.

Rummler, G., and A. Brache. *Improving Performance: How to Manage the White Space on the Organization Chart.* San Francisco: Jossey-Bass, 1990.

Stolovich, H.D., and E.J. Keeps. *Handbook of Human Performance Technology: A Comprehensive Guide for Analyzing and Solving Performance Problems in Organizations.* San Francisco: Jossey-Bass, 1992.

Swanson, R.A. *Analysis for Improving Performance: Tools for Diagnosing Organizations & Documenting Workplace Expertise.* San Francisco: Berrett-Koehler, 1994.

Zemke, R., and T. Kramlinger. "Looking at Performance." In *Figuring Things Out.* Reading, Massachusetts: Addison-Wesley, 1982.

Bricker, B. "Basics of Performance Technology." No. 9211 (out of print).

Carr, D.A. "How to Facilitate." No. 9406.

Callahan, M. "From Training to Performance Consulting." No. 9702.

———. "The Role of the Performance Intervention Specialist." No. 9714.

Kirrane, Diane. "The Role of the Performance Needs Analyst." No. 9713.

Koehle, Deborah. "The Role of the Performance Change Manager." No. 9715.

Gill, S. "Linking Training to Performance Goals." No. 9606 (revised 1998).

Robinson, D.G., and J.C. Robinson. "Measuring Affective and Behavioral Objectives." No. 9110 (revised 1997).

———. "Tracking Operational Results." No. 9112.

## Job Aid

# Evaluator Competencies Assessment

Below are three evaluation competencies and enabling outputs for the role of evaluator. Read each entry and assess your rate of competency and ability to produce enabling and terminal outputs as: satisfactory, needs improvement, or unsatisfactory. In the space provided list the ways you plan to improve your competency level for the particular area—examples may include becoming active in professional associations, reading journals and periodicals in the field, working on projects with others, and observing and emulating role models.

|  | Satisfactory | Needs Improvement | Unsatisfactory |
|---|:---:|:---:|:---:|
| **Performance Gap Evaluation Skills** | | | |
| Measure or help others to measure the difference between actual performance and ideal performance. | ☐ | ☐ | ☐ |
| **Enabling Outputs** | | | |
| HPI evaluation products: | | | |
| objectives | ☐ | ☐ | ☐ |
| designs and plans | ☐ | ☐ | ☐ |
| instruments | ☐ | ☐ | ☐ |
| findings | ☐ | ☐ | ☐ |
| conclusions | ☐ | ☐ | ☐ |
| recommendations | ☐ | ☐ | ☐ |
| Pre- and post-measures of worker performance | ☐ | ☐ | ☐ |
| Reports to management and employees on the outcomes | ☐ | ☐ | ☐ |
| **Terminal Outputs** | | | |
| Written and/or oral reports to the following parties about the interventions' progress: | | | |
| participants and stakeholders | ☐ | ☐ | ☐ |
| the organization | ☐ | ☐ | ☐ |
| work groups or teams | ☐ | ☐ | ☐ |
| management | ☐ | ☐ | ☐ |

**Evaluator Competencies Assessment, continued**

|  | Satisfactory | Needs Improvement | Unsatisfactory |
|---|---|---|---|
| Written and/or oral reports to the following parties about performance: |  |  |  |
| the organization | ☐ | ☐ | ☐ |
| work groups or teams | ☐ | ☐ | ☐ |
| management | ☐ | ☐ | ☐ |

I will improve my performance gap evaluation skills by taking the following actions:

1. _____

2. _____

3. _____

4. _____

5. _____

## Evaluate Results Against Organizational Goals

| | | | |
|---|---|---|---|
| Assess how well the results of a human performance improvement intervention match intentions. | ☐ | ☐ | ☐ |

**Enabling Outputs**

Being able to link HPI interventions to the following:

| | | | |
|---|---|---|---|
| other organizational change efforts | ☐ | ☐ | ☐ |
| other interventions | ☐ | ☐ | ☐ |
| organizational plans, goals, and objectives | ☐ | ☐ | ☐ |
| organizational and business needs | ☐ | ☐ | ☐ |

## Job Aid

### Evaluator Competencies Assessment, continued

|  | Satisfactory | Needs Improvement | Unsatisfactory |
|---|---|---|---|

I will improve my ability to evaluate results against organizational goals by taking the following actions:

1. _____

2. _____

3. _____

4. _____

5. _____

## Standard Setting Skills

Measure desired results of:

| | Satisfactory | Needs Improvement | Unsatisfactory |
|---|---|---|---|
| organizations | ☐ | ☐ | ☐ |
| processes | ☐ | ☐ | ☐ |
| individuals | ☐ | ☐ | ☐ |
| Help others to establish and measure work expectations | ☐ | ☐ | ☐ |

### Enabling Outputs

| | Satisfactory | Needs Improvement | Unsatisfactory |
|---|---|---|---|
| work standards and expectations established and communicated | ☐ | ☐ | ☐ |

I will improve my standard setting skills by taking the following actions:

1. _____

2. _____

3. _____

4. _____

5. _____

# Linking Training to Performance Goals

Issue 9606

**A U T H O R :**

**Stephen J. Gill, Ph.D.**
Consultant for Human
    Performance Improvement
2402 Vinewood Boulevard
Ann Arbor, MI 48104
Tel: 734.665.7728
Fax: 734.665.7864

Steve Gill has over 20 years'
experience in training needs
analysis and performance
improvement programs. He
served as a professor at The
University of Michigan and has
written more than 35 articles,
books, and manuals on needs
analysis and program evaluation.
He coauthored *The Learning
Alliance: Systems Thinking in
Human Resource Development.*

**Editorial Staff for 9606**

**Editor**
Mary O'Neill


**Revised 1998**

**Editor**
Cat Sharpe

**Contributing Editor**
Ann Bruen

# Linking Training to Performance Goals

# Linking Training to Performance Goals

Performance is the most critical issue in training and development today. Companies of all types and sizes are aspiring to become high performance organizations. What is meant by performance and performance improvement? Simply put, performance is measured in terms of progress toward specific business goals. To claim that performance has improved, there must be measurable change according to the yardsticks the company has set for itself. Performance is also related to how employees achieve the targeted results. The behaviors and on-the-job processes—from the simplest task to the most complex corporate strategy—are examined for high returns.

How does this emphasis on performance influence training and the training practitioner? It is certain that people who are fluent in performance improvement methods will have an advantage over those who are not. A trainer can begin to make a shift toward the performance mindset by linking training to performance goals. This *Info-line* discusses new ways to approach training with performance in mind.

## Why Performance?

The recent drive for results has come about due to a variety of pressures, such as local and global competition. Previously, location, superior technology, and price would give companies a competitive advantage. But now a rival can reach the same locations with the same technology at a lower cost from just about anywhere in the world. Companies also are facing pressure from an increasing demand for higher-quality products and services. It is more and more difficult to stay ahead on the basis of quality products, however, because everyone has access to the same technology. Companies can still gain an advantage with exceptional service to customers, but this requires a considerable investment in training for employees.

Still another pressure is financial. Financial pressures from government regulation, stockholders, and the world economy are forcing all companies to do more with less—that is, fewer dollars and fewer people while still meeting greater financial

goals. Moreover, the advent of empowerment means employees have higher expectations of organizations. Employees expect a high quality work life and more involvement in workplace decisions. They want to participate in shaping their future by contributing to the improvement of products and processes.

In her article "Reinventing the Profession," Patricia Galagan says that this trend toward high performance work organizations requires that the human resource development profession reinvent itself. She writes that trainers must shift from a focus on "training and development activities (input) to the performance of individuals and organizations (output)." Dana Gaines Robinson and James Robinson, in their book *Performance Consulting,* say that trainers can help companies focus on performance by moving beyond the traditional training role to one of performance consulting. These two roles are compared in the sidebar that follows.

This change to a performance focus means that training practitioners must think differently about their work than they have for the past century. (For more information, see *Info-line* No. 9702, "From Training to Performance Consulting.") When jobs were made up of a defined set of repetitive tasks, training was relatively simple and could be accomplished in one short program or even done on site by a somewhat more experienced employee. A positive reaction to the training or a gain in knowledge was enough.

But in today's environment of complex jobs and sophisticated technology, training events—attending a workshop, seminar, or meeting; reading a book, report, or professional paper; listening to an audiocassette; or watching a videotape or tele-conferenced seminar—are not sufficient to meet the performance improvement needs of employees. Even achieving the instructional objectives of a training event does not necessarily result in the level of performance needed by the organization. High performance companies no longer have the luxury of providing training without performance improvement, nor performance improvement without the achievement of strategic goals.

## Making the Shift

How can you help your organization make the shift from training to performance? Start by accepting these beliefs about the training function:

- The business of a trainer in an organization is to help the organization be successful.

- Continual individual performance improvement is necessary if the organization is to achieve its strategic goals.

- Performance improvement is the result of a learning process, not isolated training events.

- Everyone in the organization is responsible for their own performance improvement and for helping others learn.

At first glance, these beliefs may seem indisputable. But they run counter to common practice. Step back from your job for a moment and examine the underlying assumptions that you and your organization make about your role, the purpose of training events, and the purpose of the training function. This self-examination is necessary for making the shift to a performance mindset. If you believe that materials heavier than air cannot fly, you won't get in an airplane. If you believe that your role is to deliver training events, you won't make the move to performance.

After changing your existing belief system to correspond with performance thinking, the next step is to form learning alliances with managers. The main purpose of a learning alliance is to make use of the knowledge of everyone in the organization. The accumulated knowledge of a company is one of its most valuable assets. This knowledge is as important to business success as is property and inventory, equipment and machines, products and services, and the loyalty of employees and customers.

Human resource development professionals can help to expand corporate knowledge by creating learning alliances between employees and their managers, between the training department and other departments, and among all of the departments of the organization. The trainer's role cannot be passive or reactive. The trainer must take a proactive role to integrate learning into all aspects of corporate life, to make everyone a learner and teacher, and to document learning for use in the future.

# Linking Training to Performance

Four principles can help your company link training to performance:

**1.** Link training events and outcomes clearly and explicitly to business needs and strategic goals.

**2.** Maintain a strong customer focus in the design, development, and implementation of all training activities.

**3.** Manage training with a systems view of performance in the organization.

**4.** Measure the training process for the purpose of continuous improvement.

In a particular training setting, one or two of the principles might figure more prominently than the others. But all four principles are integral to the process, and each should be included when trying to make the shift.

## Principle One: Goal Linkage

This principle holds that training will result in performance when it is linked to important business goals. The performance linkage diagram that follows illustrates this relationship. A focus on the employee is represented by the top arrows: An employee (for example, a supervisor) learns skills, knowledge, and attitudes (say, coaching), that hopefully result in needed workplace behaviors (performance feedback to subordinate), leading to certain outputs (subordinate knows areas for improvement), which might contribute to key business processes (reduced errors in work), and achievement of departmental goals (lower costs), which could help the company achieve its overall goals (lowest cost producer).

Each of these types of outcomes has an effect on employee performance, but the maximum effect comes from integrating all of the goals of the system. For instance, the first outcome—training for new skills and knowledge—is crucial, but unless the other components of this model are fully integrated, it will not result in high performance. You might work with a group to help them learn about teams and teamwork, but if

# Traditional Trainer Role vs. Performance Consultant Role

The following table is reprinted from *Performance Consulting: Moving Beyond Training* by Dana Gaines Robinson and James C. Robinson.

| Element | Traditional Trainer Role | Performance Consultant Role |
|---|---|---|
| Focus | Identifies and addresses learning needs of people. | Identifies and addresses performance needs of people. |
| Output | Produces structured learning experiences such as training programs, self-paced packages, and computer-based training programs. Views training as an end; if people have learned, then the desired outputs from the traditional trainer role have been achieved. | Provides services that assist in changing or improving performance. These can include training services but should also include formation of performance models (that is, performance needed to achieve business goals) and guidance in addressing work environment obstacles. Views training as a means to an end. People must transfer what they learn to the job. Only when performance has changed in the desired direction has the output from the performance consultant role been completed. |
| Accountability | Held accountable for training activity. Measures include number of participant days, instructor days, and courses. Frequently, the axiom under which this role operates is "More is better." | Held accountable for establishing and maintaining partnerships with managers and others in the organization. The contribution to improving the performance of people in the organization is measured. |
| Measures | Training evaluations are completed for participant reaction and learning. | The results of training and nontraining actions are measured for performance change and cost benefit. |
| Assessments | Assessments typically identify only the *training* needs of employees. | Assessments are completed to determine *performance* gaps and the reasons for these gaps; in this manner the work environment's readiness to support required performance is identified. |
| Relationship to Organizational Goals | Training function is viewed as a cost (not an investment). Training programs and services have a limited, acknowledged linkage to business goals. | The function is viewed as producing measurable results, such as cost savings. Completed work has a high linkage to the organization's goal. |

*Copyright 1995 by Dana Gaines Robinson and James C. Robinson. All rights reserved. Reprinted with permission.*

those employees and their supervisors do not see how that will make a difference in their products and services, motivation to apply the new learning and retain that learning will be minimal.

To ensure the outcomes are linked to performance goals, the training practitioner should start with an end goal in mind and build from there. This is illustrated by the lower set of arrows shown in the diagram. Given the strategic business goals, what are the departmental goals? Given the departmental goals, what should be the business process objectives, the job outputs, and the job behaviors? And given the needed job behaviors, what skills, knowledge, and attitudes are needed by each

employee? This grasping of the strategic business goals and working back to individual or team performance is known as "mapping." Strategic mapping is a technique for analyzing and then showing the relationship that links an employee's learning goals to the ultimate goals of the company.

Of course, this is only a model for understanding and applying the first principle. Organizations are never this simple. The constant interaction among all of these elements makes the process of improving employee performance dynamic, and calls for creativity and resourcefulness. For example, you may discover that when newly trained employees try to achieve a particular objective, the objective

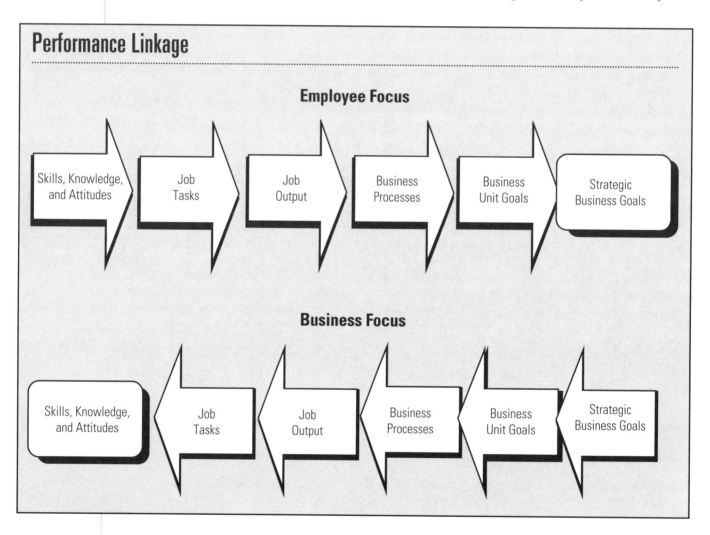

## Performance Linkage

### Employee Focus

Skills, Knowledge, and Attitudes → Job Tasks → Job Output → Business Processes → Business Unit Goals → Strategic Business Goals

### Business Focus

Skills, Knowledge, and Attitudes ← Job Tasks ← Job Output ← Business Processes ← Business Unit Goals ← Strategic Business Goals

proves to be unrealistic. The objective may be based on an outmoded business process (for example, paper-based tracking of production figures). You may have to help managers modify the business process before you can decide on the appropriate set of skills to be taught.

Linkages between employee job classification and business goals can change dramatically over time. Analyze each element of the model, but be prepared to constantly modify the content based on the current needs of the organization.

Show managers the linkages that tie training outcomes to the achievement of business goals. Engage them in the process of performance improvement. This involvement will make them valuable allies in the process. They can provide the information that you need to develop performance training, get the support you need to deliver and reinforce the training, and help ensure that the training remains relevant over the long term.

## Principle Two: Customer Focus

You will achieve performance only when the performance improvement process is meeting the needs of its customers. Anyone who benefits from the performance training process is a customer of that process. The value of the process is derived from meeting customers' needs. The most high-tech, interactive, fun, and instructionally sound training program has no value to the company unless it helps its customers improve individual and company performance.

Customers can be internal or external to the company. An important point to keep in mind is that employee learning should benefit the many different internal and external customers, not just trainees.

The list in the box on this page shows the different kinds of training customers and what they typically expect from training programs. As you can see, the expectations vary and cannot possibly be fulfilled by training events that are isolated from the business of the organization. These expectations will change as customers become more aware of what they need to be successful.

## Customers of Training and Their Expectations

**Supervisors expect:**
- less need for close supervision of subordinates
- improved job performance of subordinates
- little or no drain on their budgets
- minimal disruption to production or service delivery
- no additional burden on their time

**Trainees expect:**
- convenience
- new skills and knowledge they can use on the job
- more success on the job
- more respect and recognition from supervisor
- training that is enjoyable and nonthreatening

**Senior management expects:**
- a financial return on their investment in training
- better employee attitudes and morale

- leverage in recruiting and retaining employees
- training that is invisible to external customers
- no additional problems
- no resource or time conflicts

**Organizational support staff (such as employment administrators, affirmative action officers, attorneys, and accountants) expect:**
- training that does not bias promotion or compensation in such a manner as to create liability
- training activities that are consistent with fairness, ethics, and organization policies

**External customers expect:**
- high-quality products and services
- no added costs due to training
- training that does not interfere with the fulfillment of their needs and wishes

Identify the customers of the performance improvement process first. Using the linkage model, ask, "Who is invested in the outcomes at each link in the process?" Then analyze each group's needs by involving representatives of those customers in a dialogue about what outcomes they want. Not everyone will be aware of their needs immediately, but through careful probing and feedback, and through involving the customers in the process of performance improvement, you will be able to uncover their true needs. For example, in an exchange with trainees about job behavior objectives, you may find that an environmental obstacle would thwart any training that takes place. They might gain the knowledge to do the job more efficiently, but faulty equipment would prevent them from translating that knowledge into action. This is the kind of information that you can obtain in a dialogue with customers of the process. The key is involvement.

To get a well-rounded perspective from all customers, you can summon different representatives into a learning alliance—an advisory group representing all of the various customers. Ask this group to review your ideas about customers and their needs. Use them to interpret needs analysis data. Have them review the linkage model and monitor progress as you use training to help achieve business goals. Maintain this customer focus by constantly thinking about solutions to performance problems that will help a particular customer take maximum advantage of his or her learning.

Some managers in Ford Motor Company have developed an approach that prioritizes the needs of the performance improvement customer. Their training must fit the "four J's":

### ■ *Just Enough*
Include only the amount and length of training that learners can absorb at a particular time given their work situation. Many hour-long bites of information have more impact than a two-day workshop.

### ■ *Just in Time*
Deliver the training when and where the learners need it to do their jobs. Don't limit the training to a regular schedule and a catalog of courses. Use on-the-job methods and new technologies to be time-relevant.

### ■ *Just the Right Content*
Give learners what they need at that particular time. Cover the topics that they can put to use in their work right away and give a lot of thought to what they can use in the next 48 hours. The content must be relevant, not just nice-to-know information.

### ■ *Just the Right People*
Make sure that the people who need the training are getting it. Don't send everyone to Excel classes because sometime they might need to know how to use a spreadsheet. This is a waste of time for the people who will not use it immediately. Involve only the people who truly have the immediate need.

## Principle Three: Systems Thinking

A system, as defined in the literature, is a network of elements that function interdependently to produce some outcome. Taking a systems approach ensures that the whole system has a greater positive impact than can be achieved by the independent effects of its parts. (For more information, see *Info-line* No. 9703, "Systems Thinking.")

Training is part of an organizational system. Training does not have independent purposes. The purposes of training are always driven by larger considerations, and the success of training is always dependent on the integration of training with other elements in the organization's system. In order to achieve high performance, you must understand the dynamic interaction of training events with the other elements of the system.

Nontraining managers control many of these elements. They control hiring, benefits, finances, business operations, quality control, engineering, management, and other functions relevant to a particular business. All of these functions affect employee performance. These nontraining managers can enhance or inhibit the effective design, development, and maintenance of the performance training process. Therefore, training must have cross-functional involvement of people external to the training process.

The performance case study opposite shows how important this cross-functional involvement is. It describes how customer service training was used to help a franchise company become better oriented toward customer service and teams. But the success of the training was dramatically affected by factors outside of the training program itself. Performance was affected by the attitude of store owners toward customer service and teamwork; whether or not employees were rewarded and recognized for applying the training on the job; whether managers in the stores provided the opportunity for employees to apply what they had learned; whether departments worked on improving their communication with one other; and the support of everyone in each store for ongoing learning and change. High performance could not be achieved without integrating all of these non-training processes in the system.

Even the training process that leads to improved performance has many interrelated elements that are critical to success. A training event is only one of these elements. Planned separately, training events have little impact on performance. But planned in conjunction with all of the other elements, high performance is likely. Plan for the

---

# Performance Case Study

A franchise company decided to use customer service to its competitive advantage, so it offered a customer service training program to its franchisees. The program aimed to do more than just build skills—it was intended to bring about real cultural change.

By most standard instructional system design criteria, the training design and delivery were excellent. But learning and the application of that learning varied greatly among the stores. Some stores achieved dramatic improvement, while other stores experienced the opposite effect—actually making their work environments worse than they were before the training. Why?

**Sabotaging success.** Many of the franchise stores were managed by owners who had "grown up in the business." They had traditional, top-down, command-and-control styles of management. The training program was designed to change the culture of the stores. In effect, the company was telling this group of store owners that they'd been doing everything wrong for 20 or more years and that they should manage their stores differently in the future. They should encourage teamwork and cooperation, and they should empower employees at all levels to make important decisions related to the customers.

Many of the old-guard store owners resisted that push. They willingly sent employees to training. But then, in effect, they sabotaged the application of what the employees learned.

They provided no time for teams to meet. They failed to encourage or even discuss empowerment within their stores. They did nothing to change the organizational structure to allow departments to communicate directly and solve problems together. They provided no rewards or recognition.

The training event had raised many employees' hopes. They expected to return to workplaces that would involve them in improving conditions for both customers and employees. When that did not happen, they became discouraged.

**A new paradigm at work.** What about the other stores, the ones that experienced dramatic improvements? Why did these stores continue to apply the training long after the training event?

In the stores that achieved results, the owners accepted the fact that they needed to change; in some cases, they were already beginning to change. They saw the training as an opportunity to involve all employees in efforts to focus on customer service.

In these stores, the owners approached learning from the perspective of the new paradigm. They communicated to employees their high expectations for the training. They integrated learning into all operations, and they approached the application of learning as an ongoing process, not a one-time program. They used the training to analyze problems and plan long-term solutions.

Everyone became involved in the vision of the owners and helped to build on that vision. The stores' successes or failures became everyone's responsibility.

*Adapted from "Shifting Gears for High Performance," by Stephen J. Gill,* Training & Development, *May 1995.*

total process. A model of the major elements of this process is shown opposite. The process is made up of four subprocesses that point to four interrelated tasks:

- Formulate training goals that are linked to business needs.

- Plan training strategies that will consistently and efficiently achieve those goals.

- Produce learning outcomes necessary for effective performance.

- Support performance improvement that will add value to products and services.

Each of these subprocesses is directly affected by the cluster of six interrelated elements that surround each subprocess on the chart. You may think of additional elements that could be in these clusters. As you can see in this model, the training event is only one of many factors that affect performance.

Look at the "needs" element in the "formulating training goals" subprocess as an example. You can see how this part of the system is interrelated with the other elements. Although it is a key element of the formulating training goals subprocess, the "needs" information affects decisions in every other part of the process. Clarity of training goals requires an understanding of the learning and performance needs of individuals and of the organization. You will learn much more about needs, however, as you plan training strategies, provide learning opportunities, and continue to support high performance on the job. As you discover more and more about needs, you can use this information to plan, deliver, and support training. Therefore, the needs analysis element is related to all of the subprocesses of high performance training.

Consider the following example:

*Your company wants to use a new suite of software products to facilitate collaboration among work group members. In initial interviews with group members, you find out how much each person knows about using this and other types of groupware. You use this information to design a training program. When you begin the program, you find*

*out more about each person's skill level. You find that some learners have less ability than they had reported, while others have more. You observe indicators of their attitudes toward the use of groupware and attitudes toward collaboration. You use this additional information to shape the training and to support the transfer of their new learning to their jobs. You also discover that even though company executives support using the software, many managers are not enthusiastic about it. You realize that you will have to add incentives for using the software, and you will have to modify the training goals and redesign the training program. This shows the interrelationship of the many elements of an organizational system.*

## Principle Four: Process Measurement

This principle is based on a broad definition of measurement. Measuring the process certainly includes looking for indicators of progress toward and achievement of performance goals. But it also includes understanding what it is about the process that helps employees learn. It includes helping employees improve and sustain their performance over time. This is the kind of information that will help the organization continually improve the process of training employees for high performance.

If your goal is to deliver an excellent training program, then you only need to measure the quality of the program itself. You can do this by answering questions such as:

- To what extent did the program follow instructional design and adult learning principles?

- What did participants like and dislike about the program?

- What new knowledge and skills did participants gain from the program?

You need make use of this information only among trainers within the training department. They are the ones who can make the necessary improvements in the program, and they are the ones who are accountable for the program in the organization.

# High Performance Training Process

### Formulating Training Goals

- Needs Assessment
- Supervisor Involvement
- Setting Learning Goals
- Team Involvement
- Linking to Strategic Goals
- Selection of Learners

### Planning Training Strategies

- Pre-training Tasks
- Supervisor Expectations
- Training Schedule
- Individual Performance
- Objectives
- Team Building
- Work Process Design

### Supporting Performance Improvement

- Supervisor Support
- Coaching
- Progress Measurement
- Tracking Performance
- Performance Incentive
- Team Support

### Producing Learning Outcomes

- Training Event
- Feedback from Supervisor
- Evaluation of Training Event
- Action Planning
- Just-in-Time Training
- Skills Practice

When you have performance goals, however, you must apply a more comprehensive set of measures and use the information in a broader way. The total training process, as described above, is what needs to be measured, and managers throughout the organization become important audiences for and users of this information.

Each of the elements and subprocesses in the performance training process model should be measured. Measure the formulating of training goals, the planning of a training strategy, the producing of learning outcomes, and the supporting of performance improvement. Measure the interaction of the elements and subprocesses with one another. For example, can *performance* goals be achieved by redesigning a *work process* instead of creating a new *training event?*

These measures do not need to be rigorous—in fact, the simpler the better. The point is to collect data (numerical and anecdotal) that help the customers of training understand the progress that employees and the organization are making toward improved performance. These customers need to know what is working well and what should be changed. If managers of a manufacturing line are presented with evidence that their behavior is a barrier to the performance improvement of employees on that line, those managers can make a decision to change.

Once you decide what needs to be measured, why it needs to be measured, and how you will use the information in the organization to achieve high performance, then you can select the appropriate method of measurement. If you are training a cross-functional group to become a high performance team, for example, you may want to do the following:

- Survey team members about their attitudes toward teamwork.

- Interview team members about the effectiveness of communication among team members.

- Observe the team members in action to measure how they get things done.

- Survey the team's internal and external customers about their perceptions of team effectiveness.

- Examine team products for indicators of quality.

The results of these measures should be reported to key stakeholders in the organization who can use the information for process improvement purposes. By bringing people into the performance improvement process, you build a sense of ownership and commitment to performance improvement. The responsibility for learning and change is shifted to the people in the organization who should have the ongoing responsibility.

You also should measure the outcomes of the training process. The most important outcomes are the goals and objectives that you mapped out while you were applying principle one: linkage. The box opposite presents a framework for matching these goals and objectives with the questions that you should be asking about these outcomes and with some potential measures of these outcomes.

The following strategies will make the measurement process useful to you and to the organization:

■ *Involve Customers*
Include input from customers in deciding what to measure and how to measure it. Ask them what they want to know and why. Ask them for their thoughts about the data collection methods that you are recommending. Ask them to help pilot these methods to see if the method will produce the information that you need. Often a workshop format that allows these stakeholders to work together as a group is useful. This process of answering measurement questions with input from key stakeholders may be more valuable to achieving performance goals than the actual data that is collected.

■ *Select the Right Measurement Method*
Choose the method of measurement only after deciding what to measure. The tendency is to use a survey to measure just about everything that has to do with training. But we have many different methods available to us. The appropriateness of the method depends on what kind of data is needed, the sources of that data, the circumstances for

collecting the data, and how the data will be used. See *Info-line* No. 9605, "How to Focus a Training Evaluation," for more information on different kinds of measurement instruments.

### ■ *Match Data to Customer Needs*

Report data that are credible to the customer. Line managers may accept the accuracy of employee interviews and focus groups, whereas senior executives may listen only to production and financial data. Know your audience so that you can collect measurement data and report findings that the key stakeholders will find convincing.

### ■ *Report Data Accurately*

Report findings so the customer can hear them. This has to do with how the information is reported. You want all of the various customers to understand your findings and be able to act on the implications. Keep it simple, relate it to the goals that are important to the particular audience, and recommend what should be done about the results.

### ■ *Assess the Measurement Process*

Measure the process as well as the outcome. Continuous improvement is achieved by regular assessment of where people are in the process of learning the skills, knowledge, and attitudes they

## Measuring Performance Improvement Outcomes

| Outcomes | Measurement Question | Measurement Method |
| --- | --- | --- |
| Employee knowledge, skills, and attitudes (KSA) | Which employees need to learn what KSAs to perform the job? What are employees' current levels of performance? | Observation, survey, simulation, knowledge test |
| Job behavior objectives | How well are employees performing the job? To what extent are they using KSAs? | Supervisor report, observation, self-report |
| Job output objectives | What are the results of each job? How could employees be more successful? | Job monitoring data, production reports, team analysis of job |
| Business process objectives | How have the job outputs contributed to the desired process improvement (for example, customer satisfaction, quality)? | Customer satisfaction survey, manager's report, key manager interviews |
| Department/unit goals | To what extent has the department/unit achieved its performance goals? | Customer survey, manager's report, key manager interviews |
| Business strategic goals | To what extent has the organization achieved its performance goals? | Quarterly and annual reports, business status reports, executive interviews |

need to achieve high performance. Adjustments to the process can be made, especially as you find out more about employees' needs and the organization becomes clearer about its goals.

### ■ Impart Useful Information

Provide just-in-time and just-enough information. Give employees only what they need, when and where they need it. Performance is maximized when people are not overwhelmed with new information, when they can relate new skills and knowledge to their work, and when they can apply the learning to a problem on the job immediately. Mentoring programs, on-the-job coaching, and job aids are a few of the methods that can be more "just in time" than classroom training.

### ■ Apply Measurement Carefully

Measure to improve the process, not to blame or punish. It is human nature to feel threatened by anything that might reveal our personal competency. When we feel threatened, we become less cooperative and less willing to improve performance. Do everything that you can to assure participants that the measures are not being used to make judgments about individuals. Then follow through on this promise. Use the data only to make changes in the training process and to plan for additional activities that will make a difference in performance.

## Putting It All Together

Now that you've read what it means to link training to performance goals, are you ready? Use the performance readiness checklist job aid at the end of this issue to assess the extent to which you have taken the steps to help your company become a high performance organization.

This checklist is based on the four principles for linking training to performance goals. You can use it to guide your training efforts. The checklist reiterates the principles and adds statements that elaborate on the principles and can be used to help you address them. These statements are exemplary, but not exhaustive. You may want to consider more indicators based on your particular situation.

Apply this checklist to a single, unified training process. The checklist can be used to guide the design of training by building a positive response to each item. It also can be used retroactively to assess conditions and the need for improvement in an existing training program. The checklist also serves as a summary of the practices covered in this *Info-line*.

Seek to optimize each of the four principles—linkage, customer focus, systems thinking, and process measurement—with respect to available resources. Do what you can, given the circumstances. If failure to adequately address even one of the principles will seriously hamper performance improvement, then the project should not proceed until a more effective plan can be created. Most often, you will find that there are interim solutions that allow you to proceed with a modest, but workable, beginning.

# References & Resources

## Articles

Barron, T. "The Road to Performance: Three Vignettes." *Technical & Skills Training,* January 1997, pp. 12-14.

Carnevale, E. "The Questions and the Answers: An Interview with Robert Mager." *Technical & Skills Training,* July 1992, pp. 14-17.

Carr, C., and L. Totzke. "The Long and Winding Path (From Instructional Technology to Performance Technology)." *Performance & Instruction,* August 1995, pp. 4-8.

Clark, R.C. "Hang Up Your Training Hat." *Training & Development,* September 1994, pp. 61-65.

Dervarics, C. "Is Good Training Performance-Based?" *Technical & Skills Training,* July 1992, pp. 9-12.

Galagan, P. "Reinventing the Profession." *Training & Development,* December 1994, pp. 20-27.

Gill, S.J. "Shifting Gears for High Performance." *Training & Development,* May 1995, pp. 24-31.

Harless, J. "Performance Technology Skills in Business: Implications for Preparation." *Performance Improvement Quarterly,* vol. 8, no. 4 (1995), pp. 75-88.

Nancy, C. "Performance-Linked Training." *Public Personnel Management,* Winter 1988, pp. 457-463.

Pucel, D.J., and J.C. Cerrito. "Integrating Selection, Training, and Performance Evaluation." *Performance Improvement Quarterly,* vol. 2, no. 4 (1989), pp. 22-29.

Regalbuto, G. "Recovery from Occupational Schizophrenia." *Training & Development,* May 1991, pp. 79-86.

Rosenheck, M. "Closing the Gap Between Training and Performance." *CBT Solutions,* May/June 1997, pp. 50-53.

Rummler, G. "In Search of the Holy Performance Grail." *Training & Development,* April 1996, pp. 26-32.

Wehrenberg, S.B. "How to Reengineer Training Functions for Time and Quality Gains." *Training Director's Forum Newsletter,* September 1994, pp. 1-3.

## Books

Bowsher, J.E. *Revolutionizing Workforce Performance: A Systems Approach to Mastery.* San Francisco: Jossey-Bass Pfeiffer, 1998.

Brache, A.P., and G.A. Rummler. *Improving Performance: Managing the White Space on the Organizational Chart.* (2nd edition). San Francisco: Jossey-Bass, 1995.

Brinkerhoff, R.O., and S.J. Gill. *The Learning Alliance.* San Francisco: Jossey-Bass, 1994.

Dubois, D.D. *Competency-Based Performance Improvement.* Amherst, Massachusetts: HRD Press, 1995.

Garratt, B. *The Learning Organization.* London: HarperCollins, 1987.

Gilbert, T.F. *Human Competence: Engineering Worthy Performance.* New York: McGraw-Hill, 1978.

Harbour, J.L. *The Basics of Performance Measurement.* New York: Quality Resources, 1997.

Harris, P. *High Performance Leadership: HRD Strategies for the New Work Culture.* (revised edition). Amherst, Massachusetts: HRD Press, 1995.

Langdon, D. *The New Language of Work.* Amherst, Massachusetts: HRD Press, 1995.

Mager, R.F., and P. Pipe. *Analyzing Performance Problems.* (3rd edition). Belmont, California: Lake Publishing Company, 1997.

Pepitone, J. *Future Training: A Roadmap for Restructuring the Training Function.* Dallas: AddVantage Learning Press, 1995.

Robinson, D.G., and J.C. Robinson. *Performance Consulting.* San Francisco: Berrett-Koehler, 1995.

Stolovitch, H.D., and E.J. Keeps. *Handbook of Human Performance Technology: A Comprehensive Guide for Analyzing and Solving Performance Problems in Organizations.* San Francisco: Jossey-Bass, 1992.

# References & Resources

## *Info-lines*

Austin, M. "Needs Assessment by Focus
Group." No. 9401 (revised 1998).

Berke, G.B. "How to Conduct a Performance Appraisal." No. 9005.

Bricker, B. "Training Basics: Basics of
Performance Technology." No. 9211
(out of print).

Callahan, M. "From Training to Performance Consulting." No. 9702.

———. "The Role of the Performance
Evaluator." No. 9803.

———. "The Role of the Performance
Intervention Specialist." No. 9714.

Carr, D.A. "How to Facilitate." No. 9406.

Garavaglia, P. "Transfer of Training:
Making Training Stick." No. 9512.

Kirrane, D. "The Role of the Performance
Needs Analyst." No. 9713.

Koehle, D. "The Role of the Performance
Change Manager." No. 9715.

Marquardt, M. "16 Steps to Becoming a
Learning Organization." No. 9602
(revised 1997).

O'Neill, M. "How To Focus a Training
Evaluation." No. 9605.

Robinson, D.G., and J.C. Robinson.
"Measuring Attitudinal and Behavioral
Objectives." No. 9110 (revised 1997).

Robinson, D.G., and J.C. Robinson. "Tracking Operational Results." No. 9112.

Sullivan, R.L. "The Transfer of Skills Training." No. 9804.

# Performance Readiness Checklist

|  | Yes | No |
|---|:---:|:---:|

**Goal Linkage—Linking training events and outcomes clearly and explicitly to business needs and strategic goals.**

| | Yes | No |
|---|:---:|:---:|
| I understand the organization's business goals and strategies. | ☐ | ☐ |
| I have mapped out the relationship between strategic goals and each of the following: knowledge and skills, job behaviors, job success indicators, and business objectives. | ☐ | ☐ |
| I have designed pre-learning, learning event, and post-learning activities that are integrated into key business processes. | ☐ | ☐ |
| I have created an iterative process of delivery, feedback, and redesign for achieving timely learning and effective changes as business goals shift. | ☐ | ☐ |
| Throughout the training process, I emphasize the links between training activities and business needs. | ☐ | ☐ |
| I provide repeated training interventions that reinforce learning over the long term. | ☐ | ☐ |

**Customer Focus—Maintaining a strong customer focus in the design, development, and implementation of all training activities.**

| | Yes | No |
|---|:---:|:---:|
| I involve all stakeholders (anyone who has a vested interest in the outcomes of learning) in the training process. | ☐ | ☐ |
| I have stakeholders validate the needs analysis, the training goals, the training design, and the link between training and business goals. | ☐ | ☐ |
| I schedule and provide learning activities in ways that fit the schedules and learning styles of training customers. | ☐ | ☐ |
| I help training customers apply learning to the workplace. | ☐ | ☐ |

**Systems Thinking—Managing training with a systems view of performance in the organization.**

| | Yes | No |
|---|:---:|:---:|
| I help everyone in the organization understand the dynamic interaction between learning and the following areas: rewards and incentives, business processes, job design, job tools, supervision, and performance assessment. | ☐ | ☐ |
| I have designed the training process so that supervisors, peers, and subordinates help trainees learn and apply that new learning. | ☐ | ☐ |
| I make learners aware of the systematic factors that will hinder or facilitate effective performance. | ☐ | ☐ |
| I have integrated learning interventions with work processes. | ☐ | ☐ |
| I encourage cross-functional collaboration before, during, and after training events. | ☐ | ☐ |

**Process Measurement—Measuring the training process for the purpose of continuous improvement.**

| | Yes | No |
|---|:---:|:---:|
| I continually measure learning and its effect on performance and on the organization and report this information to key stakeholders. | ☐ | ☐ |
| I help stakeholders use training data to review and modify training goals and the training process. | ☐ | ☐ |
| I teach trainees how to assess their own learning and the transfer of that learning. | ☐ | ☐ |
| I monitor the transfer of knowledge and skills to the workplace. | ☐ | ☐ |
| I assess any impediments to the application of learning and report this information to key stakeholders. | ☐ | ☐ |